BLUES
INSIDER

BLUES INSIDER

A QUARTER OF A CENTURY WITH BIRMINGHAM CITY

KEITH DIXON

FOREWORDS BY BARRY FRY AND TREVOR FRANCIS

First published by Pitch Publishing, 2017

Pitch Publishing
A2 Yeoman Gate
Yeoman Way
Worthing
Sussex
BN13 3QZ
www.pitchpublishing.co.uk
info@pitchpublishing.co.uk

ISBN 978-1-78531-285-4

Typesetting and origination by Pitch Publishing

Printed in the UK by Bell & Bain, Glasgow, Scotland

Contents

Acknowledgements 7

Introduction 9

Preface 13

Foreword by Trevor Francis 15

Foreword by Barry Fry 19

Contributor Credits 23

Sponsoring The Blues 37

Samesh Kumar's Empire Collapses 45

The Administrator's Diary 55

Roldvale Buys The Blues 80

David Gold and David Sullivan 91

Karren Brady .105

Commercial Matters 118

Blues Magazine 125

The Bluenose Executive Lunch Club 133

Former Players' Association and Birmingham City
    All-Stars 138

An Author 149

In the Press 169

Academy Scout 190

Chinese Crackers 197

Project Jack 210

Did You Know That? 224

Stadium Project 232

Behind the Numbers 236

Bibliography 252

Acknowledgements

I DEDICATE this book to my family; Julie, Holly, Harry, Matt, Ben, Caleb and Amy – all my love.

My thanks go to all the people that have helped in the production of this book:

Jane and Paul Camillin of Pitch Publishing for getting it edited, proofread, printed and published. Also thanks to Jane and Paul for showing faith in me as a new writer to their business.

All my friends who contributed to the book, in no particular order: Mike Wiseman, Michael Dunford, Malcolm Page, Colin Burke, Ben Dixon and Colin Tattum.

Special thanks go to Trevor Francis and Barry Fry for writing the forewords. To have the two most iconic Blues favourites contributing this way is beyond my original expectations.

To Bernie Chetwynd, a neighbour and friend, who gave me access to his extensive library of football books.

Thanks to Mike O'Brien, my archivist, for the time he spent in his library (attic) searching for some of my illustrations.

Also thanks to Phil Johnson, Paul Woolridge and Tim Mulqueen who during a business trip to Stuttgart in October 2015, spent a hair-raising journey on the autobahn coming up with potential subjects for inclusion in the book.

Introduction

BLUES INSIDER – A Quarter Of A Century With Birmingham City is my fascinating catalogue of what has gone on behind the scenes at Birmingham City Football Club in the past 25 years. A lifelong Bluenose for over 60 years, I am writing about my love for the club which has taken me into a whole host of areas not normally accessed by fans, with the intention to try and improve the club's fortunes both on and off the pitch. Whether I have been successful or not is revealed within the pages of this unique book – which is a personal history and nothing more.

Along the way I have experienced many amazing things related to the workings of the club as well as making friends with many of the club's personalities, on the field as well as off it.

Prior to the writing of *Blues Insider – A Quarter Of A Century With Birmingham City,* all the revealing stories included in the book have been kept private, either locked away in the files in my home study or at the back of my mind.

After years of standing on the terraces I decided to use my business acumen and knowledge to learn more about the club and its operations. After becoming a corporate hospitality supporter, I persuaded my company at the time to become sponsor of the club.

The details of the sponsorship deal are revealed together with the reasons why Triton Showers wanted to be associated with professional football, the negotiating skills of Samesh Kumar and his family, the chaos surrounding the administration of the business and the characters that were holding it together in spite of everything. If you thought it was bad on the pitch, it was worse in the backrooms.

During this time the Kumars went into administration and as I tried to buy their shares and therefore own the club, I became friends with the administrator and included in the book is his day-by-day diary of the whole process prior to David Sullivan's company buying the shares.

The chapter 'Roldvale buys the Blues' reveals the details behind the sale, including the names of the parties interested in the club, whether they were serious contenders or the equivalent of tyre kickers, and how the sales process culminated in an offer for the club.

My dealings with Karren Brady, David Sullivan and David Gold make lively reading and give an insight into their characters and approach to business and life. The book reveals the early signs of the talent that Karren possessed as a 23-year-old, which has taken her through an incredible career that so far sees her as vice-chair of a Premier League club and a baroness.

Many senior figures associated with Birmingham City have contributed to *Blues Insider* including Colin Tattum, the journalist who covered the Blues for the local newspaper before becoming in recent times the club's head of media and communications; Mike Wiseman, the current honorary vice-president of the club; former chief executive officer Michael Dunford; administrator Colin Burke; Malcolm Page, an ex-player and Former Players' Association committee member; and my son Ben, who worked in the commercial department during the reign of Perry Deakin. They all talk candidly about their involvement behind the scenes.

I will tell you about my contacts with Carson Yeung, Panos Pavlakis and the new owners Trillion Trophy Asia

INTRODUCTION

(TTA). I reveal my offer to Peter Suen of TTA to provide a corporate governance team for six months at no cost to TTA.

Through my creation, the Bluenose Executive Lunch Club and my involvement with the Birmingham City All-Stars and the Former Players' Association I relate the stories revealed by a number of ex-players including Joe Gallagher, Ian Clarkson, Paul Tait, Tony Want, Kenny Burns and many, many more.

My connection with the playing side of the club is evidenced by getting the two most iconic personalities of Blues' history to write forewords for the book; Trevor Francis and Barry Fry.

Get to understand how the academy system worked, as I operated as a scout for several years in the south Staffordshire area. What the recruitment officers were looking for, how the prospective new players were assessed together with how the scouts were trained and remunerated.

Through the writing of a number of books on the Blues, I have become a spokesman for the supporters and the chapter 'In the Press' records my involvement with both the local and national media, commenting on promotion to the Premier League, a 12-point plan to improve the game and a revealing insight into the self-inflicted PR disasters created by David Gold and David Sullivan.

My articles in *Blues Magazine* resulted in me meeting many of my heroes of yesteryear and they too reveal their inside stories. See my catalogue of tales from Ken Leek, Bert Murray, Fred Pickering, Colin Green, Jimmy Harris, Brian Sharples and a host more.

Raising money for charity resulted in a number of events being organised with legends such as Bertie Auld and Barry Fry and all facts behind the scenes are revealed, such as who drinks lager by the pints before moving on to vodka.

I have been involved in four biographies about the lives of Midlands legends; Gil Merrick, Jackie Sewell, Bobby Thomson and Tom Ross, although only two made the bookshelves with my name as author. Find out the reasons why in this fascinating and insightful chapter.

The book culminates in a significant project as I headed up a consortium to attempt to buy the Blues from Birmingham International Holdings. It was a complicated and difficult process which ultimately failed but the detail behind 'Project Jack' is compelling stuff for a Blues supporter.

Forget match results, players' appearances, goals scored, transfers and loan deals as all that information is available online. This book tells tales that are not on the internet because they have never been told before. This is my passion for the club I have supported since I was eight, a club which has never won the league title, never held aloft the FA Cup, never qualified for the Champions League but still enjoys incredible loyalty from its fans, who like me believe that one day things will get better.

Blues Insider – A Quarter Of A Century With Birmingham City gives those supporters, with its revelations of what goes on behind the scenes, even more reasons to dream that dream.

An illustration of myself and my four children by Matt Dixon

Preface

AT THE age of 69 I still get the same feelings as I approach our ground as I did on my first visit which was on Christmas Day 1955 (yes, the players forfeited their festive fayre for a game of football in those days), Blues at home to Nottingham Forest in front of a crowd of 33,500. I remember the crowd more than the match, which was the same for my children Matt, Ben, Holly and Harry when I took them to St Andrew's for the first time just like my father had taken me. Surprise, surprise we lost the Forest game 1-0 in a season when we came first in the Second Division to gain promotion to the First Division. The team that day was: Merrick, Hall, Green, Boyd, Smith, Warhurst, Astall, Lane, Brown, Murphy, Govan.

Being a Blues fan in those days was a family thing. I was a Bluenose because my great-grandfather was one and I was determined that I would give my children the chance to follow in his footsteps.

Matt and Ben experienced a 1-0 victory on 27 March 1982 over Brighton & Hove Albion in front of a crowd of 13,324 that saw Mick Harford hit the winner on his debut in a team of Wealands, Langan, Hawker, Stevenson, Scott, Curbishley, Dillon, Evans, Harford, Broadhurst, Van Mierlo.

Holly and Harry enjoyed a 5-1 thrashing of Crewe Alexandra on 30 August 1999 when a crowd of of 24,085 witnessed Michael Johnson, McCarthy, Furlong, Holdsworth and Ndlovu score after Blues went 1-0 down after four minutes. The team was: Poole, Rowett, Holdsworth, M. Johnson, Grainger, McCarthy, Hughes, O'Connor, Lazaridis, A. Johnson, Furlong.

On 22 February 2004 my daughter and I were invited to Villa Park by a then client of mine and we assumed it was for some corporate hospitality. It was my first visit to Aston Villa even though I was 57 years of age and I was not pleased to find out that our tickets were for two seats in the Doug Ellis Stand. We had spent 85 minutes among Villa fans, sitting on our hands to prevent any overt pleasure from the performance. When we left Blues were losing 2-1. As we approached our car we heard a cheer and the other early leavers passed on the news that Birmingham had equalised in the final minute. Imagine how difficult it was to look disappointed.

Those feelings I mentioned earlier are of an unbridled enthusiasm, a churning in the stomach of expectation and the excitement and hope that today the Blues will deliver. So often that enthusiasm, expectation, excitement and hope got lost as Blues underperformed once more.

To be a Bluenose requires a special personality, one that can conquer all disappointments and still be back refreshed for the following match to cheer on our heroes.

Foreword by Trevor Francis

For his foreword, I asked Trevor to reflect on his past 25 years in football…

I WAS pleased to be asked to write the foreword for *Blues Insider – A Quarter Of A Century With Birmingham City* because although Plymouth Argyle is my hometown club I moved to Birmingham as a 15-year-old boy and spent nearly ten years playing for them, and later returned to St Andrew's in 1996 for a five-and-a-half-year stint as manager. I still live in the area so I guess I am an adopted 'Brummie'.

In the period covered by the book the Premier League has changed the financial landscape for professional footballers and England has become the place to be for top-rated international players. That was not the case in the early 1980s when Italy was the place to be for both football and financial reasons.

If the Premier League had existed then I probably would not have gone to Italy and would have missed out on five great years with Sampdoria and Atalanta. In those days there was a restriction on foreign players; only two per club, which was me plus Liam Brady for my first two years at Sampdoria and Graeme Souness for years three and four – what midfielders they were!

Today's Premier League is not the greatest league in Europe in terms of world-class players; for me it is La Liga in Spain. No player in the Premier League has the goalscoring ability of either Lionel Messi of Barcelona (312 league goals in 348 appearances) or Cristiano Ronaldo (260 in 236) at the time of writing.

Having said that, I do believe that the Premier League is the most exciting league in the world but for technical ability La Liga and the Bundesliga are ahead of us.

I took over from Ron Atkinson at Sheffield Wednesday as player-manager during the 1991/92 season and therefore was involved in the inaugural Premier League campaign. As I was improving the team by signing players of the quality of Chris Waddle, Chris Woods, Andy Sinton and Des Walker, it became more and more difficult to justify selecting myself in the squad. This restricted the games I played before I retired just prior to my 40th birthday.

In my first season at Hillsborough we finished third in the league, which in 2015/16 was worth £95m to Tottenham Hotspur. In 1993 we made the finals of the FA Cup and the League Cup, losing both to Arsenal, but the managerial pressures experienced by Premier League bosses today were starting to build up and in 1995 I was sacked when we finished 13th, a position which earned Watford in the 2015/16 season the handsome sum of £74.1m!

The 'inside stories' which Keith relates in his book remind me of my behind-the-scenes dealings with Birmingham City: persuading Steve Bruce to leave Manchester United and become captain as well as securing the signatures of Barry Horne, Gary Ablett, Mike Newell and Paul Furlong; reviving the academy system with the support of the likes of Bob Latchford and Brian Eastick; securing a new training facility at Wast Hills, West Heath plus the Worthington Cup Final and play-off disappointments.

I have had a fabulous last 25 years, with the inevitable ups and downs of being involved in the wonderful world of professional football and they are reflected in the recent past for Birmingham City and Keith Dixon, as evidenced in this book.

Enjoy the book and Keep Right On!

Foreword by Barry Fry

WHEN KEITH texted me to see if I would write this foreword, I replied 'Keith, I'll be delighted to do a foreword for your book, ring me anytime Thanks Baz'

Well he called me on 1 July while I was away pre-season in Portugal with Peterborough United, we had the briefest of chats and here we are – great stuff!

Why am I delighted to write this foreword? Because I love the football club (and still keep in touch via the Former Players' Association for whom Keith and I have organised some good charity 'dos' over the years) but most of all I was delighted because I love you Bluenoses!

Managing Birmingham City was a dream for me, nothing like the nightmare you could have imagined. It started with breakfast with Karren (Brady) at the Birmingham Hyatt Hotel, when I turned up not only with Ed Stein, who she was expecting but also Dave Howell, my player-coach from Southend United. He never played for the club but his appointment was one of the reasons it cost Birmingham £125,000 for their illegal approach to me and the boys.

It ended the day after we won the Birmingham Senior Cup for the first time in 17 years, beating our friendly rivals Aston Villa 2-0. The next morning, Jack Wiseman had told me that I had got the sack. After I asked when it had happened, Jack and Alan Jones told me, 'Two weeks ago.'

Nobody had told me. I rang David Sullivan, but he didn't take my call so I just left a message saying, 'Thanks a million for giving me the opportunity of managing a great club like Birmingham City for the last two and a half years. Good luck!'

One minute later our home telephone rang. Kristine, my wife, picked it up and said, 'It's David Sullivan for you.' 'Hello, David.' 'I got your message,' he said. 'That's very nice.' 'Yes,' I said, 'and I meant it. I understand that you want Trevor Francis back. He is God at St Andrew's.' And we parted ways.

But back to the Bluenoses. My first home game was against Charlton Athletic (18 December 1993) and a crowd of 13,714 turned up, so whatever you might be thinking but it meant a lot to me because the attendance at the previous home game had been less than 6,000! Not long after that we had a holiday fixture against West Bromwich Albion and the pitch was covered in snow. I said to Alan Jones, the club secretary, that regrettably there would be no chance of playing the game and he said, 'You watch.' His intention, he said, was to have an announcement made by the local radio station that help was required to clear the pitch. I thought there was no chance because it required an army to clear it, not just a handful of fans.

Within half an hour, I was watching in astonishment as, indeed, a veritable army arrived. With a burning desire to get the match on they used every implement they could bring to hand to clear every flake of snow. The game kicked off at the scheduled time of 3pm on 28 December 1993, in front of a giant crowd of 28,228, the biggest First Division attendance of the season. We won 2-1.

I'm 71 and have had a great career in football. I started as an England Schoolboy, playing six times and scoring five goals before leaving school and signing for Manchester United where I stayed for four years. Because of injury, I had to pack up my playing career at the ripe old age of 29 so I went into management with Dunstable. The genius that is George Best guested for me on four occasions and I attracted Jeff Astle, the King of West Bromwich Albion, and he helped me gain promotion in my first season in management.

When I was first appointed manager of the Blues, it was December and we were bottom of the league. By the time the end of the season arrived, we had won eight, drawn seven and only lost 15 of our games.

I will never forget the scenes at Tranmere Rovers on the final day of the season, when we started the day fourth from bottom. We won the game but got relegated and there were 5,000 Bluenoses inside and outside of the ground, all in fancy dress. They carried me shoulder-high. You would have thought I had won the FA Cup, not dropped down a place in the table and been relegated on goal difference.

The following season I made a promise, a very bold prediction, that Birmingham City would win the double and despite some iffy times, we did. We won the league on the final day at Huddersfield. This was the year that only the champions would be promoted due to the reformation of the divisional structures following the implementation of the Premier League three seasons previously. We went to Wembley and won the Auto Windscreens Trophy in front of 78,000 supporters, which was a bigger attendance than Liverpool in the League Cup Final that year. Of the crowd, 55,000 were Bluenoses. What a fantastic day out.

In 1994/95 we also had a great FA Cup run, playing Liverpool at home in front of 25,000 and drawing and then going to Anfield and drawing again after extra time. We got a standing ovation, but we lost 2-0 on penalties. In the press conference after, the media were very complimentary about our performance but asked me for an explanation on us missing all four penalties. I replied, 'I have got such a great team spirit here at St Andrew's that once one of the players missed a penalty, nobody wanted him to feel bad, so we all missed them.'

We also got to the semi-final of the Coca-Cola Cup, losing to Leeds United, and my under-21 team won the Capital League and cup, which helped me develop a lot of players. When I first went to St Andrew's they had a first team and a reserve team in the Pontins League, but players coming out of the youth team could not cope with the leap so I introduced an under-21 team. That is why I ended up with 46 players.

I had a first team of 14 players, a reserve team of 14 and an under-21 group of 14. In fact, I would have made it to 50 players but Karren Brady returned home from holiday three days early and scuppered the deals!

I was in charge of 156 games of which 68 were wins, 44 were losses and 44 draws, which according to Keith gives me a win percentage of 39.86, but in one of the Birmingham City history books, I have a win ratio of 55 per cent. Forget the stats though, I've worked with some 'colourful' employers; Keith Cheeseman at Dunstable, Stan Flashman at Barnet and David Sullivan but even though I have been sacked from every management job I have had, I bear no grudges because life's too short and you should live every day as if it is your last.

Enjoy the book and Keep Right On!
Barry 'Baz' Fry

Contributor Credits

Colin Burke

I met up with Colin at Piccolini's in West Didsbury on Monday 26 September 2016 for a lunchtime chat about his time at the Blues.

So who is Colin Burke? He was a manager with Leonard Curtis & Partners in 1992. Still none the wiser?

Leonard Curtis & Partners were the appointed joint administration receivers of BRS Kumar, owners of 84 per cent of Birmingham City Football Club.

So in answer to the question, he was the person given the responsibility on 1 November 1992 to sell the Kumars' shares in the club, which he successfully achieved at 4.20pm on Friday 5 March 1993. But more of that later.

Colin was the perfect choice for this onerous role: he knew Birmingham, he knew football and he knew how to get a good deal for all parties concerned.

From 1973 to 1975 he lived in Birmingham, a teacher at Oakley Road School in Small Heath for a year before moving to an administrative post at Birmingham Poly. An Evertonian by birth, during his two years in the city he was a regular on the Kop at St Andrew's and distinctly remembers joining in with the defiant chant of that time, 'We're going to stay up!'

So how fortuitous it was that 17 years later a Blues fan was appointed as the person responsible for selling the Kumars' shares. As Colin puts it, 'The antithesis of the gypsy curse!'

Colin had more than a spectator's interest in football. He recounts how in 1981 Ken Bates, Freddie Pye and Bobby Charlton took a controlling interest in Wigan Athletic AFC. At the time I had a well-paid job heading up the student services at Manchester Polytechnic, but when my pal Bobby asked me to take a £3,500 drop in salary to become Wigan's club secretary/CEO, I decided to give it a go.

Larry Lloyd was the manager, Chris Lawler was his number two, and I have to admit I really enjoyed the job. We did some good work in terms of developing the ground and the team and I looked forward to a career in the sport. But then one day in 1983 Ken Bates announced that he'd bought Chelsea and everything changed at the Latics. As the rules don't allow anyone to own more than one club, Mr Bates eventually sold his shares to a group of local business people, who kept me on just long enough to pick my brains and get to know the ropes, and then they saw me off.

So, as I've often recounted, Ken Bates joined the board at Chelsea, Freddie Pye joined the board at Manchester City, Bobby Charlton joined the board at Manchester United and I joined the dole queue in West Didsbury.

This was Thatcher's Britain and jobs were hard to come by up north, and I was doing anything that came my way; tree felling, bar tending, driving, anything. So I was pleased when Bobby Charlton's accountant, Ruben Kay, offered me what he thought would be just three days' work in his insolvency section, dealing with creditors' enquiries at a greengrocers called Harrops which was in receivership.

Well, three days turned into three decades and I discovered that I had a knack for insolvency, mainly because it's really all about dealing with people (be they staff, directors, creditors or whoever) rather than accountancy, and I'd always enjoyed interacting with all kinds of people. As I say, over 30 years later I'm still at it having eventually progressed to starting my own firm in 1995.

I had a clear objective regarding my time at Birmingham City and that was that if people remembered Colin Burke and/or Leonard Curtis years after then it would be because we hadn't done a good job for the fans and the club. Football fans have long memories and are slow to forgive – just ask the administrators of Glasgow Rangers if you don't believe me. Well I'm sure if, in the style of BBC's *Pointless,* we were to ask 100 Bluenoses to name the firm or individual who dealt with the sale of the club in those traumatic months, not one would name Lennies or me.

Selling the Blues was a reminder to me that, whatever the circumstances, never lose your sense of humour, and always get your priorities right. On the day the sale was announced the telephones were 'red hot' and I was taking consecutive calls from every national and local newspaper, plus all the television and radio stations. 'Yes I can confirm the sale,' I was repeating constantly.' 'Yes that was a certain Karren Brady I met with on Wednesday,' I repeated for the tenth time. My PA Juliana had all the calls queuing up nicely, then she came on and said, 'I've got Sky Sports on line three, BRMB Radio on four, but your wife's just come on, on five.' Getting my priorities right, I let my wife jump the queue. 'Be quick,' I said, 'it's bedlam here.' Appreciating the situation, she got straight to the point. 'Do you want chips or mashed potatoes with your sausages tonight?'

In 1995 I set up my own insolvency practice, Milner Boardman and Partners, and have handled the administration of over 2,000 companies. I have been approached by a number of football clubs to handle their affairs; I have always refused. I want my record to remain at 'played one, won one'. Oh, and I listened in to the last game of the season on the radio up in Manchester, and heard the glorious refrain go up on the Kop,

'And now you're going to believe us, we're going to stay up.'

Look out for more of Colin's stories elsewhere in the book.

Colin Tattum

I met Colin Tattum, head of media and communications for Birmingham City, at the Wast Hills Training Ground on Friday 22 July 2016. Since joining the Blues, Colin has been very supportive to me and was instrumental in getting my book *The Leaders – Birmingham City* awarded the status of 'the official publication for the 140th anniversary of the formation of BCFC.' Nothing is too much trouble for Colin and on this occasion I asked him to get a shirt signed by the first-team squad plus also pass on a royalty cheque to Paul Robinson for our book, *Robbo – Unsung Hero.* For all your help Colin, thanks so much.

We met over a cup of tea in the parents' room, which is predominantly for the parents of the academy students, and on the wall is the following notice: 'The task of becoming a professional footballer is a lifestyle choice not a single training session or game.'

Here are Colin's recollections:

I joined the *Birmingham Mail* on work experience in 1988 and eventually was taken on as a news reporter. My first job as a sports journalist was covering Wolverhampton Wanderers before I took over the Blues coverage in the 1989/90 season. This means I have spent most of my working life covering the Blues and to leave the newspaper world in 2014 was a wrench but it was getting extremely frustrating the way newspapers were going and how the company that owns the *Mail* were treating journalists and the way they wanted sport and the local clubs covered.

When Andy Walker left Blues to join the media team at the Football Association, the club approached me and we both agreed this was the ideal time to make the move, which had been mooted a couple of times previously.

I made my 'debut' on 29 November 2014. This was my first official day and it coincided with a game against Nottingham Forest which was christened 'Trevor Francis Day'.

The Premier League has resulted in an improvement in the standard and quality of players over the past 25 years. To me every game is built like an event in itself – it can be gripping, regardless of the teams playing. The fitness, professionalism and attention to detail now demonstrated by every Premier League team is extraordinary although I suspect people feel the game has lost its soul a little.

The Championship is a league that is underrated; it is so unpredictable and in every game either team more often than not has a spell of dominance. Matches are always in the balance and I enjoy both top-flight football and the Football League for these reasons.

My long-term connection with the Blues has meant I have come into contact with many of the personalities associated with the club.

Barry Fry was a larger-than-life character who has a real passion for the game. He was brought in deliberately by David Sullivan and the Gold brothers to breathe life into Blues and make them interesting again not just locally, but nationwide.

Steve Bruce spent more than eight years at Blues, as a player then manager. He forged a genuine affection for the club. Guiding Blues to promotion after such a long wait, and a hat-trick of play-off near-misses, was a memorable feat and one, I believe, he looks back upon as arguably his best achievement, given all the circumstances, and the atmosphere it generated at that time.

When David Gold was trying to get Trevor Francis to come back to the club after he had resigned after a sponsor abused his son, Steve was still captain. Steve was back in the north-east on that day and a constant stream of phonecalls kept coming my way from him asking, 'Is he staying or going?' Steve was always keen on becoming Blues manager as he knows how big the club is, and could become.

My job has given me unique access to the players, managers and staff of Birmingham City. Some of my favourite memories are times when you would just chat football with them, talk about their experiences in the game and their views. Some of the anecdotes, evenings out and tours I have been on have been hugely enjoyable and some not for public consumption!

Mick Mills was compelling company when talking about football and Alex McLeish, although he knows leaving the way he did and where he went was a mistake with the benefit of hindsight, was fantastic company and had time for everybody. He was a genuine guy.

Stand-out events were the pre-season tours to Ireland in the late 1980s and early 90s. They were just crazy and sometimes resembled a drinking festival occasionally interrupted by training sessions, which were conducted on parks pitches. I recall having to drive the minibus Blues received for winning the Leyland DAF Cup in 1991 around Ireland, packed to the rafters with players and kit. I remember Simon Sturridge had to lay across the kit skips and bags of balls to find some room and he was desperately trying not to slide about as I attempted to negotiate various winding roads.

Winning the Carling Cup at Wembley in 2011 is the most memorable and emotional experience I have had with the Blues. Having been at the sharp end and close to the club for so long, it was something akin to a pinnacle as the local reporter.

I was asked by the club to put some words together for a two-minute slot Blues had for the Wembley big screen. I came up with the 'This is Our Time' theme over a glass or two of red one night and put it to Chris Coles and Chris Alcock, then part of the audio-visual team at the club. They produced the video, Glynn Purnell did the voiceover and it was one of my proudest moments to see and hear the reaction the video got when it was played pre-match at Wembley. The roar at the end was spine-tingling and, hopefully, we had managed to capture the mood of what the final meant to Blues, the supporters, and how we weren't there just to make up the numbers.

Still thinking about that day now, it has an effect on you. As we win a major trophy roughly once every 48 years, it's hard to explain to those who aren't Blues supporters just exactly what the whole final, the day, the way Blues got to Wembley, encapsulated for us all.

Aspects of my role include bridging any gap between the players and the media – and by extension the fans – and I approach it with a very simple mantra: I treat people as I would wish to be treated myself. I always tried to be fair when I was reporting, without ever losing a constructively critical eye – and that has created a level of trust which cannot be gained overnight. I have had various players and managers of Blues over the years compliment me on my approach and I believe I built up a level of understanding and respect, which is a two-way thing as well.

One of my favourite players and characters was Christophe Dugarry, who loved the adulation he received from the crowd, which he never enjoyed in France. He was signed over a cuppa and a rich tea biscuit by Steve Bruce and asked to come in and do a job – lead and keep the club up, and try and help move Blues on. It appealed to him.

After he signed a two-year contract following that thrilling impact he made during the initial loan, I always remember him asking me in pre-season, very seriously, with that Gallic shrug of his, 'What will I do when it gets dark at four o'clock in the afternoon?' He wasn't used to our long, dark winters in his chateau in Bordeaux!

Rather ironically, my final match report for the *Birmingham Mail* was on the humiliation of an 8-0 home defeat to Bournemouth. I remember thinking to myself as the goals were going in, 'Great, how do I report this before joining the club?' After I handed in my resignation at the *Mail* no one was aware of where I was going to go four weeks later, so I did have a wry smile to myself at the thought of that match because of personal circumstances but that was it, the defeat left me like many Blues fans fuming, in all honesty.

How the future unfolds now promises to be equally as fascinating. As we prepare for another ownership change, chronicling the fortunes of Blues from the outside or helping to create them from the inside, there's never a dull moment when it comes to this great club of ours.

Look out for more of Colin's stories elsewhere in the book.

Malcolm Page

I met Malcolm on Tuesday 6 September 2016 at Olton Golf Club, where he is a long-standing member. It was a glorious day and we sat outside overlooking the impressive course being filmed by Gary James and his crew from Big Centre TV. Our interview was ultimately screened on 26 September at 6.30pm on *Big Sports Extra*.

Malcolm and I have been friends for over 20 years and when he was playing he was one of my heroes due to his 100 per cent attitude and total commitment to the shirt. I was delighted when he agreed to contribute to this book. 'Malc' made over 390 appearances in all competitions and scored eight league goals. For 25 years he was the most capped Blues player with 28 full caps until he was overtaken by Australia's Stan Lazaridis in 2005.

Malcolm recalls:

I love the Blues fans, when I was a player I would love it when they came up to me to chat about football and Blues. When my playing career ended, after a brief spell at Oxford United, I devoted the next ten years to developing my career outside of football and therefore could not get to games. I truly missed going down to St Andrew's. However, since 1992 I have attended matches on a regular basis and still enjoy meeting and chatting with the fans as both an ex-player and a supporter.

The club look after the former players these days and will always provide a ticket for a game. That wasn't always the case during the David Sullivan era, where there was no respect for the club's heritage evidenced by an incident when ex-players' contracts etc. were found in a skip at the ground. Whenever I go to the ground I am always impressed by the non-playing staff in terms of their professionalism, their capability and enthusiasm. They do an excellent job in promoting the club and generating commercial revenues. You are always greeted with a smile which makes me happy to be at St Andrew's.

Gil Merrick was a major influence on my career and I was pleased to write the foreword to Keith's biography on the great man in 2009. He signed me as an apprentice and guided me to a long and enjoyable career with Blues, the club got under my skin at the age of 15 and I have never wanted to leave from that day forward. It has always been part of my life and I can't escape it.

Although times have changed the basics of being a good footballer have not changed: You need to find space, control the ball, move the ball on to a team-mate and then move yourself into a new space. It's the way it has always been. The apprentice scheme was good for young players as you had to learn your trade, you had to listen and face the reality of working even if it was sweeping the terraces or cleaning the first-teamers' boots. I hope the youngsters of today appreciate the terrific opportunity they have been given.

Scoring goals, although I didn't get many, did not fill me with great joy; what did give me great satisfaction was performing well as an individual (I always knew when I played badly) and the team getting the right results.

The Premier League has been good for football because apart from their financial well-being the players are extremely well looked after in every aspect of the game e.g. fitness, nutrition, relaxation techniques etc. I don't like the dominance of the big clubs due to the money but I guess every fan would like to be in that position.

The introduction of foreign players has made it more difficult for home-grown talent. I think the authorities have got it wrong when they stipulate the number of British players in the squads, it should be the other way round.

Football is definitely better in terms of techniques, coaching and improved surfaces. Sometimes I think I could still play on the quality of pitches available today!

The club has been through some challenging times in recent years but despite that, and it does amaze me, we have carried on and are still carrying on!

If I had my way I would love to see competitive football played without the influence of money, where clubs had to develop their own players – but that's just wishful thinking.

The best thing about my being a Bluenose is the association with the ex-players and the fans. When I'm asked what is the worst thing about being a Bluenose I always answer, 'Nothing.'

Michael Dunford
Michael Dunford is a 'football man' and it all started for him when another 'football man' – the great Brian Clough

– invited Michael to join the Derby County box office at the age of 16 on 20 July 1969. Michael remembers the date as it coincided with man landing on the Moon. As he puts it, 'Man landed on the Moon and I went into orbit!'

Gone were his plans to be a draughtsman and he stayed for 25 years, eventually becoming club/company secretary, general manager and chief executive officer. He remembers his first wage packet being £8 per week with an extra £5 for working Sundays, so needless to say he worked a lot of Sundays!

In November 1994 he joined Everton, initially as company/ club secretary before being appointed chief executive officer in 1999. During his ten-year period at Goodison Park he was the club's representative with UEFA, the FA and the Premier League. He then spent four years as CEO at Plymouth Argyle from January 2005 to July 2009 before joining Birmingham City in October 2009, resigning six months later. After a spell working as a member of the judicial panel of the Football Association he became a director/CEO at Crawley Town where he stayed for 30 months before leaving in March 2016 when the board resigned to facilitate the takeover of the club by Turkish businessman Ziya Eren.

Michael recalls:
Football's a funny old game, I think that's been said before but here are a few examples to justify that statement.

At 9.30am on my first day at Everton in November 1994 the manager at the time, Mike Walker, came to my office to wish me luck and at the same time announced he had just been sacked! Wow, welcome to the Premier League.

Bill Kenwright had negotiated a deal for Andy Gray to be installed as Everton manager following the departure of Joe Royle in 1997. Andy appeared extremely excited at the prospect of returning to manage a club where the supporters absolutely adored him. Overnight however he had a change of heart and before Bill could announce his appointment, Sky had persuaded Andy to remain. Just maybe they had made him an offer he could not refuse! That's football, a deal is not a deal until the ink is dry on the contract.

The Blues are well blessed with being able to call upon the assistance of the Former Players' Association to support their matchday activities. Kevan Broadhurst, Tom Ross and the committee do a fantastic job linking legends of yesteryear with the club's ambitions for the future.

Football is a very small world and I keep an eagle eye out on the fortunes of the Blues. Better days will surely return, my God those Blues fans have thick skin but their loyalty to the top side in Birmingham must never be taken for granted! Keep right on and keep it blue!

Look out for more of Michael's stories elsewhere in the book.

Mike Wiseman

I have known Mike Wiseman for over 25 years and recognise him as a true gentleman and a devoted fan of Birmingham City, so it was no surprise that he agreed to meet with me to talk about the club which we both love with such passion.

Typical of Mike, he invited me to join him for lunch on 11 July 2016 at the Little Italy restaurant on the Stratford Road in Shirley, which is close to his office. We enjoyed a great couple of hours chatting about his experiences and of course he refused my offer to pay the bill!

Here are Mike's recollections:
David Sullivan invited David and Ralph Gold to join him as owners of Birmingham City FC and they all immediately invested in the team, which prevented us from being relegated that season. They also undertook all the responsibilities for

the rebuilding of half of the ground so as to comply with the new regulations on stadium safety.

In the first proper season they had control, a very poor run of results enforced a change of manager with Terry Cooper stepping down to be replaced by Barry Fry. Barry's tenure of the club was simply unforgettable as there was literally never a dull moment with even the most ardent fan struggling to keep up to date on player comings and goings!

Barry unfortunately could not prevent us from being relegated that season and still to this day talks about the game at Tranmere Rovers, where our fate was sealed despite winning 2-1. The massive Blues following, many of whom were attired in fancy dress, invaded the pitch and hoisted him in the air as if we had won the league! This amazing loyalty was repaid the next season as not only did we get promoted but we also won the AutoWindscreens Trophy at Wembley by beating Carlisle 1-0 in front of nearly 55,000 Blues fans.

Life in the First Division proved much tougher and after a very poor run of results at the end of the season David Sullivan and Karren Brady decided it was time for a change and replaced Barry with Trevor Francis. Karren was never a person to avoid a tough decision and it has come as no surprise to me how successful she has become since she left Blues as even now a lot of good practices she introduced at the club are still rigidly adhered to. I also owe her personally as she gave me the opportunity to become a director of the club which is every supporter's dream job.

I don't think there can be any argument that Birmingham City FC, with the benefit of several seasons in the Premier League, is a vastly improved entity as a result of the tenure of David Sullivan, Karren Brady and the Gold brothers.

Read more of Mike's stories elsewhere in the book.

1

Sponsoring The Blues

I JOINED Triton Showers in June 1984 as general sales manager when the company was turning over £6.1m and our PBT (Profit Before Tax) was £617k. When I was promoted to the board as sales director in December 1985 our turnover had grown to £11.8m and our PBT was £2.2m.

At that point in the company's development the shareholders decided to 'float' the business on the Stock Exchange via the merchant bankers, Kleinwort Benson. Regrettably the Initial Public Offering never materialised due to some negative information regarding a previous business activity of the chairman not being declared until the 11th hour. The purpose of the float was to maximise shareholder value and therefore we were all extremely disappointed.

In 1987 Triton plc was acquired by Norcros plc for £47.5m with it effectively paying an 11-times multiple on our profits (1987/88 financial year results declared sales at £17.3m and our PBT at £4.3m). My fellow directors left the business upon the deal being finalised and I was promoted to the position of managing director with a clear remit from the holding company (Norcros) to grow the business from its already successful base. Not an easy challenge!

It became clear that the business was not going to grow quickly enough by making and selling electric showers and therefore I established a diversification strategy. The vision was agreed as wishing to become 'No.1 in Healthy Living Products'.

So Triton began to supply to the market new products such as mixer valves (non-electric showers), bathroom accessories, shower pumps, power showers and do-it-yourself spa baths, alongside a second electric shower brand, Aquatron.

During this period Triton had been declared by Audits Great Britain to be the number one shower brand in the UK with a market share in 1992 of 41 per cent. We needed to grow awareness of our brand with our consumers. One idea proposed by our marketing team was to enter the world of sponsorship initially at a local level, which we did with Nuneaton Borough Football Club, Warwickshire Society of Referees (rugby union) and round four of the FIA Sports Car World Championship at Donington Park – as you have probably deduced Triton was also based in Nuneaton.

Having learned some important lessons about what sponsorship entailed we decided to embark on a national sponsorship deal, and I had to present to the Triton board my proposal to sponsor Birmingham City. This was a difficult task as apart from my sales director there were no football fans on the board, let alone any Blues fans. Suffice it to say I was mandated by the board to look at football sponsorship as a method of raising awareness of our valuable consumer brand. At that time our turnover was £33.9m with a PBT of £8.8m.

Mike Wiseman recalls:

'Prior to the 1992/93 season 83 per cent of the Blues' shares were owned by Ken Wheldon, who by trade was a scrap metal dealer and a very scrupulous man as we never owed HMRC a penny! Ken paid an undisclosed sum for Keith Coombes's shareholding plus he took over the loans and guarantees Keith had made to keep the business afloat with the club probably about £2m in debt at the time. The other directors at the time – Jasper Carrott, Neville Bosworth and Derek Coombes – refused to convert their loans into shares but my father Jack decided to back Ken and converted his loans in return for eight per cent of the company's shareholding. John Wardle of Edge Ellison, who at the time was a very well respected professional advisor, told my father that it was a bad business decision but Jack wanted to support Birmingham City.

'Eventually Ken sold his shares to the Kumars for around £500,000 and Jack was disappointed not to be involved in the negotiations.

'Samesh Kumar and his two brothers, Ramesh and Bimal, treated Jack with a lot of respect and achieved some success when the Blues won the Leyland DAF Trophy in 1991 at Wembley and achieved promotion too. Unfortunately this all came to a halt when their main retail business went into receivership after the collapse of Bank of Credit & Commerce International.

'The Kumars literally disappeared overnight which left a horrible situation for the club as no one could get a cheque signed, and the accounting records were not in good order, which made it very difficult to ascertain the Blues' financial situation. The board of directors was hastily reconvened with Jack becoming chairman, Alan Jones (club secretary), Bill Caldwell (general manager) and Terry Cooper (first team manager) becoming directors, with myself as a chartered accountant acting as an advisor.'

The company sponsorship deal was for three years and the cost was £100,000 to be paid by three annual payments of £33,333.33. Samesh promised to call me after the deal was approved by his family, and the call came on a Sunday evening. As well as confirming the deal he asked if the first- and second-year payments could be paid up front. I refused as that was not what had been agreed but to me it was the first sign that the Kumars had serious cash issues.

The deal presented exceptional value and was unanimously approved by the Triton plc board which was made up of Peter Warry (chairman), John Hodgkinson (sales director), Peter Dimeloe (marketing director), Rex Walker (finance director) and Graham Tiso (production director).

The content of the sponsorship included:

- Shirt sponsorship for all teams
- A full-page advertisement in all home matchday programmes
- An executive box for ten in the Old Stand for all home games
- Rename of the Railway End Stand to 'Triton showers – healthy living products'
- Two boardroom passes for all home games
- A game on the St Andrew's pitch for the Triton team against the Birmingham City All-Stars
- Support for the Triton heathy living programme – we produced an eight-page brochure which included the following introduction, *'On behalf of Birmingham City Football Club and Triton plc I would like to introduce you to our Healthy Living Programme. You may be wondering why Triton have teamed up with Birmingham City FC, well apart from the players requiring frequent showers after training sessions and matches, the image of the healthy footballer*

is one well in keeping with Triton's range of healthy living products. Based in the Midlands, both Birmingham City FC and Triton have relied on the support of the local community both for our customers and for our workforce. As partners we believe that now is the time to put something back into the community. Our Healthy Living Programme is designed to tour schools and youth organisations in the local community helping young people to understand the benefits of a healthy lifestyle. Our aim is to work in partnership with schools and other organisations to promote all aspects of Healthy Living. Mindful of the demands of such things as the National Curriculum we have designed our scheme to be flexible in order to accommodate the requirements of each group we visit. I hope you will read this brochure about our scheme, and having done so recognise its value by making use of the programme in your organisation. Keith A Dixon Managing Director Triton plc' The brochure included a photograph of Ian Rodgerson in the shower, plus images of Paul Mardon, John Gayle, Paul Fenwick, John Frain and Graham Potter together with our community welfare officer Shaun Edwards.

We also agreed to refurbish the home dressing room showers and the toilets in the corporate areas. There was also a success clause whereby we would pay £150,000 if the club was promoted to the Premier League and a further £10,000 for each televised game.

Overall Triton's sponsorship of the Blues was a success and circumstances favoured us in terms of promotional value. There was great publicity surrounding the deal at the outset and usually that's as much press coverage as a sponsor is going to generate but then the Kumars went into liquidation, which was big news on the sports and business pages. Soon after that, the club was sold to David Sullivan, and a 23-year-old female managing director arrived in a short skirt and blue Porsche so we were all over the local and national press!

Still to this day I, and indirectly Triton, get the blame for the first-team shirt which had been designed by Samesh. It was a royal blue shirt with supposedly shower drops in the colours of the Indian flag. When we had our match against the Birmingham City All-Stars they refused to wear it, opting instead for the reserve team strip. Perhaps it was the matching shorts and socks that proved too much?

It was 5 August 1992 and as part of the sponsorship deal we had agreed to play Tom Ross's All Stars as pre-match entertainment before the Blues' pre-season friendly against John Toshack's Real Sociedad.

The Triton side was augmented by second-half substitute Willie Carr (the former Coventry City player), who was a supplier's representative but it made little impression as we were beaten 4-1. I only played for the first 45 minutes and didn't stop sweating until hours after the game ended. The lushness of the grass and the thrill of playing on the 'hallowed turf' was too much for me and my well below average football skills found new depths of inadequacy.

I played in the number three shirt and was supposed to mark Brian 'Harry' Roberts. Just getting close to him was a challenge too far for me. To say I was overcome by the occasion would be an understatement. I can understand how some players fail to turn up at major finals because they are more interested in what's going on around the fixture instead of focussing on their game.

Included in the All-Stars were Tony Want, Colin Brazier, Malcolm Page, Terry Cooper, Des Bremner, Kevan Broadhurst, Ian Atkins, Brian Roberts, Keith Bertschin and Tony Evans plus rotating substitutes in the form of Tom Ross, Brian Caswell and Ramesh Kumar.

It is worth noting that to fill an executive box of ten for every home game with customers and suppliers is an impossible task and therefore it invariably got full of family members and friends – I believe it's the same today.

I also championed a 'Save the Terraces' campaign. The programme read:

TODAY'S MATCH SPONSOR
FAREWELL TO THE TERRACES!
Keith Dixon, Triton M.D. announces the Triton Terrace Supporters Challenge – and offers you the chance to win a trip to the World Cup!

Soon we reach the end of an era when we say farewell to the Terraces at St Andrew's. While in many ways this will be a sad day, Triton wants to celebrate this occasion by honouring the Terraces, and the supporters who have stood there, year in, year out, in all weathers.

Today we are launching a special competition – The Triton Terrace Supporters Challenge – which will run throughout the season. We are trying to find the one supporter whom we believe personifies all that is good about football, and the tradition of the terraces.

That winner will receive a trip to the World Cup in the USA in 1994. Two runners-up will receive BCFC season tickets.

All we want you to do today is complete the coupon.

Questions will be posed in match programmes over the next few months. The winner and runners-up will be announced at the Bolton Wanderers match on Saturday 30 April – the Blues' last home game. Good luck!

Some interesting moments in the first year of our deal:

The first league match under the Triton sponsorship was at home to Notts County. It was played on Sunday 16 August and Blues won 1-0. If you possess the programme then you have a rare oddity as the date is misprinted on the cover as Wednesday 12 August 1992! Little did we know then the impact broadcasting deals would have on the traditional Saturday at 3pm kick-off.

On 4 November 1992 I used one of our boardroom passes after the Newcastle United game. one of the Newcastle directors was fast asleep for the whole encounter and it was not a quiet environment for the reason that it was the first time I had seen Barry Fry in post-match action. Terry Cooper had a quiet manner and was very respectful of the required atmosphere in the boardroom but Baz was different. The door flew open and he burst in reflecting on our 3-2 defeat in his traditional loud style, including a few profanities.

All through this turmoil the Newcastle guy remained asleep and Sir John Hall, who was I believe chairman of the Magpies, had to check that he wasn't dead.

Paul Mardon, who we signed from Bristol City in 1991, had a recurring injury so the advice from the medical team was to try cycling. Joan Hill, the marketing manager of Blues who always went the 'extra mile' to ensure that our sponsorship delivered top value, saw the opportunity for some publicity for the sponsor and the potential to get Paul fit. In Nuneaton there was an independent bicycle retailer, Chris Dodds & Son, which was run by the son, Walter, who most people called Chris! Joan spoke to me to explain her idea and on 13 November Triton presented Paul with a bike but whether it worked or not, only he will know.

2

Samesh Kumar's Empire Collapses

IN NOVEMBER 1992 the Kumars' business went into receivership and by the end of the season the Blues' board comprised of David Sullivan (owner), Jack Wiseman (chairman), Karren Brady (managing director) and Terry Cooper (manager).

I first met Samesh Kumar in the summer of 1992 when I was considering the idea of Triton Showers becoming the shirt sponsors of the Blues. He was an extremely likeable man and very keen to make his investment in Birmingham City pay off. He and his brothers ran a clothing business based in Manchester and therefore were not particularly well-equipped to run a football club.

Lou Macari wrote in his book *Football, My Life*, 'I'm not sure the chairman properly understood the game he was in. The Kumar brothers had a clothing business in Manchester. They were new to football. They thought they could treat players like commodities, not as people with mortgages to pay. Samesh thought he could wheel and deal like he did in business. He was a nice fella, a good fella. I got on well with him, still do to this day. But I could not work with him.'

Colin Tattum recalls, 'One of the early owners I dealt with, Samesh Kumar, was young, enthusiastic and I always felt a frustrated footballer. When he was in charge the relationship between the club and the media was not great and there were a few clashes, one time resulting in him calling me a "liar and writing untruths" to my face but refusing to repeat the same in public.'

In 1992 Birmingham City Football Club was a wholly-owned subsidiary of BRS Kumar Brothers Limited, who owned 84 per cent of the club. In 1992 the Kumar brothers' bankers, BCCI, collapsed.

In the *Manchester Evening News* on 3 March 2009 the following report appeared:

> The Bank of Credit and Commerce International was a major international bank founded in 1972 by Agha Hasan Abedi, a Pakistani financier. The Bank was registered in Luxembourg with head offices in Karachi and London. Within a decade BCCI touched its peak. It operated in 78 countries, had over 400 branches, and had assets in excess of US$ 20 billion, making it the 7th largest private bank in the world by assets.
>
> BCCI came under the scrutiny of numerous financial regulators and intelligence agencies in the 1980s due to concerns that it was poorly regulated. Subsequent investigations revealed that it was involved in massive money laundering and other financial crimes and illegally gained a controlling interest in a major American bank. BCCI became the focus of a massive regulatory battle in 1991 and on July 5 of that year customs and bank regulators in seven countries raided and locked down the records of its branch offices.

Investigators in the US and the UK revealed that BCCI had been 'set up deliberately to avoid centralized regulatory review, and operated extensively in bank secrecy jurisdictions. Its affairs were extraordinarily complex. Its officers were sophisticated international bankers whose apparent objective was to keep their affairs secret, to commit fraud on a massive scale, and to avoid detection'.

The liquidators, Deloitte & Touche filed a lawsuit against Price Waterhouse and Ernst & Young – the bank's auditors – which was settled for $175 million in 1998. A further lawsuit against the ruling Sheikh of Abu Dhabi, a major shareholder, was launched in 1999 for approximately $400 million. BCCI creditors also instituted a $1 billion suit against the Bank of England as a regulatory body. After a nine-year struggle, due to the Bank's statutory immunity, the case went to trial in January 2004. However, in November 2005, Deloitte persuaded creditor Abu Dhabi to drop its claims against the Bank of England, except for a claim for return of its deposits, in that Abu Dhabi owned 77 per cent of the bank shares at closing, and was therefore also facing a major lawsuit. To date liquidators have recovered about 75 per cent of the creditors' lost money. Over a decade after its liquidation, its activities were still not completely understood. Among others hit were top Manchester 'rag trade' group Kumar Brothers International which went into receivership.

BCCI had lent considerable sums of money to Kumar shortly before it crashed, and liquidators subsequently put the Kumar companies into receivership, under pressure from creditors to recover money. The group was one of the biggest business success stories of the 1980s, growing from nothing into a £30m turnover group specialising in selling women's and casual wear.

The group's brand was Mark One, which had its flagship store in the old Bull Ring of Birmingham and was the Blues' shirt sponsor from 1989 to 1992. Ian Clarkson, a Blues player from 1988 to 1993 who made 136 appearances without scoring, remembers:

'I can recall back in 1993 when there was prolonged newspaper speculation over who would replace Samesh Kumar. Thankfully for the club, David Sullivan and the Gold brothers arrived and the rest is history as they rescued a sinking ship and turned it around.

'However, it is a million miles from the day Samesh Kumar and his brothers – Ramesh and Bimal – arrived on the scene back in 1989. Ken Wheldon had left the building with the club set to be relegated to the third tier of English football for the first time in their history when in breezed Kumar.

'Bear in mind that every other Friday every player used to queue up at St Andrew's until about four o'clock before Wheldon finally allowed the wages to be handed out. This usually involved around 40 players hanging round the main offices getting increasingly fractious, which wasn't ideal preparation for a game on Saturday.

'Kumar's new approach appeared to be better, with payment straight into the bank and new training kit and for an initial 12 months the garden looked rosy.

'He definitely believed in a hands-on approach, which involved being "one of the lads".

'It all started promisingly enough with the dressing rooms receiving a lick of paint but initial talks over a contract were a worry when his opening gambit was, "I used to play a bit!" What this meant was he had played on a Sunday morning so felt in a good position to tell you all your faults before offering you a deal!

'The initial signs were good with a bit of cash being made available and a feel-good factor returned but his insistence that he "could play a bit" was always a concern.

'I can vividly remember a Christmas bash that was organised at the Cobden Hotel on the Hagley Road, Birmingham, and the lads had indulged in a few drinks. The dance floor was full and Samesh arrived and decided to throw a few shapes but was collared by Paul Tait who proceeded to dance about a centimetre from the chairman's face as a hard core tune blared out of the stereo!

'It was hilarious as Samesh looked uncomfortable but tried to smile and be "one of the lads". However, he didn't want to be anyone's friend when a huge row erupted over the bonuses before we played in the Leyland DAF Final at Wembley.

'Four months earlier he had held a meeting asking the players what they felt about manager Dave Mackay and two hours later he [Mackay] had gone! So when he called another meeting before our Wembley final against Tranmere

Rovers no one was particularly receptive. Bearing in mind that all the bonuses for the earlier rounds of the Leyland DAF competition were around £20 a win.

'That was fair enough, as the crowds weren't huge, but suddenly he was telling us it was £1,000 a man if we beat Brentford in the area final. So imagine our surprise when our pay packets contained about £85 for the victory.

'He came into the dressing room and spun a cock and bull story about the bonus sheet saying that we were entitled to £1,000 between us. However, Dean Peer – who wouldn't normally say boo to a goose – had a bonus sheet in his kit bag and the chairman was banged to rights.

'Kumar exploded with a wave of expletives and proceeded to verbally lay into every player and tell us all our faults and that we weren't worth anywhere near that amount. It was obvious then that Lou Macari and Samesh weren't bosom buddies as he asked Lou to back him up and the manager said, "This has got nothing to do with me."

'Our pay packet for the final at Wembley was to include a £2,000 appearance pay-out but Kumar loved a bargain so we compromised. He paid us the full whack for our area final victory but said he wouldn't pay us a penny at Wembley unless we won. The rest is history and he was true to his word as we received our win bonus.

'Don't get me wrong, Kumar had some good ideas and the fact he lent John Gayle his plush car after scoring the winner at Wembley was a sign of good faith. He was a personable bloke and always wore rose-tinted spectacles – unless he was discussing your contract!

'We also achieved promotion the following season with Terry Cooper in charge but the supporters seemed to know more than us. On our pre-season tour of Ireland a group of supporters wore anti-Kumar t-shirts and there was a feeling something was about to give.

'We sported the worst kit in living memory at the start of the 1992/93 season and were struggling at the bottom of the First Division when the roof caved in. Apparently, the club was in a dire financial state.

'There was no emotional farewell from the chairman as we all read the headlines in the *Evening Mail* that Blues were broke. Samesh resurfaced at Cardiff a few years later and I spoke to him when Northampton played them and he was still a smooth operator. There were positives from the Kumar regime but in hindsight, there were never huge finances available.

'We trained at a variety of venues during his tenure at the club and Wast Hills looked a vastly different place to how it is today.

'The last time I saw Samesh was at a Birmingham City Historical Society evening where he spoke at length about his spell in charge of Blues and he was a good raconteur. He still maintained the club wasn't in as bad a state as it was painted when he left but Samesh always did have the gift of the gab.

'A Wembley final and a promotion during Kumar's reign means that it could be deemed a success.'

During my time behind the scenes with the Blues I have only met two non-players who got into our conversation as early as possible the comment, 'I used to play a bit!' One was Samesh and the other was Perry Deakin, the former commercial manager and for a very short time director, but more of him elsewhere in the book.

After the sale of the club to David Sullivan the whereabouts of a Porsche 4x4 vehicle was unknown but sure enough it turned up in a locked compound in the London area!

Samesh re-emerged as chairman of Cardiff City where he was a director from 7 July 1995 to 18 June 2003, together with Joan Hill, who acted as a director from 7 July 1995 to 25 July 1999.

Summing things up, it is probably fair to say that Kumar's biggest problem is that he's too nice. Everyone likes him, thinks he's trying his best and all that, it's just that he never appeared to have any money.

Joan died on 21 May 2013 at the age of 66 from ovarian cancer. She was a close friend of Samesh and worked with him at Birmingham and Cardiff before re-joining Peterborough United, where she had started her football career in 1983 to become one of the first women in commercial football.

When I first met Joan she was the glue that kept the Kumars' reign at Birmingham in one piece with her personality and caring attitude. To celebrate the sponsorship she bought my two young children individual money boxes which are still on the mantelpiece at home. She was the driving force behind the marketing of the club and was a great ambassador at all times.

Unlike the Kumar brothers she had been around football all of her life and understood the ins and outs of the game, which helped her sell the club to local and national businesses.

Colin Burke recalls:

'Anyway, in 1991 I was head-hunted into a national firm, Leonard Curtis & Partners ("Lennies", as we called it) and within 12 months I had my highest profile case, namely to sell the Kumars' shares in Birmingham City Football Club. A major factor in my being allocated the job was that I knew and understood how the professional game worked. I knew the staff at the Football League really well, having regularly made up the numbers in their cricket team. (How many people's claim to fame is to have played cricket for the Football League?)

'This was important because, unlike in other jobs where you'd sell a business within a few weeks, the sale of the Blues was going to take months, and the football authorities had to be happy that the club could survive financially and fulfil its fixtures during that period. You have to remember that the club was not, repeat not, in administration or receivership; rather the company that owned most of its shares was in receivership, but that is very different from the club itself being in any insolvent procedure. Put it this way, BRS Kumar plc could have owned shares in Marks and Spencer, but that wouldn't mean M&S was bust. So we had the job of keeping the club going in order to sell its majority shareholding to raise cash for the creditors of BRS Kumar.

'Now without getting too technical, selling the shares of a plc is a far more complicated process than selling a business out of receivership. Stock Exchange rules are very demanding in order to ensure that all parties are treated fairly;

consequently a primary issue in the proposed sale was the preparation of the audited accounts so that prospective purchasers could see exactly what they were buying.

'The preparation of the accounts was exceptionally long-winded for a number of reasons, so instead of a quick "in-out-sell-be-gone" that we were used to, for five long months the club had to be run on a day-to-day basis, the shares put up for sale, offers invited and considered, and eventually contracts issued once the financial statements were finalised – and all the time everybody was keeping an eye out on our league position.

'When it came to the ongoing running of the club, a problem we had was that the chairman and vice-chairman were the brothers Kumar. Their participation was immediately terminated and, fortuitously, we had the father and son team of Jack and Mike Wiseman already on the board and ready to step up to the challenge and take on the senior positions. I'd known Jack from my Wigan days and quickly assessed that Michael was a very capable and trustworthy chap, so we were confident that they would steer the ship on a steady course. Equally, club secretary Alan Jones proved to be a real asset in what were certainly trying times at St Andrew's.'

3

The Administrator's Diary

*Diary relating to Birmingham City FC plc kept by
C.T. Burke, Manager, Leonard Curtis & Partners*

The contents of CTB's diary are reproduced intact other
than I have chosen to delete addresses and telephone
numbers as a matter of courtesy to the people involved.

1992

Monday 1 November

C. MacMillan & S.D. Swaden appointed Joint Admin
Receivers of BRS Kumar, owners of 84 per cent of
Birmingham City – No announcement.

Wednesday 3 November

Birmingham City 2 Newcastle 3

Thursday 4 November

Press release planned for 4.30pm.

C. MacM approves a courtesy call to the Football League
by CTB at 2pm. CTB spoke to Chris Whalley and said
Receivers have no plans to interfere.

Friday 5 November

1pm On the instigation of DS, CTB made contact with Alan Jones, Secretary of BCFC assures him of position (no change, no interference, Receivers will want to sell shares, maybe Mr Kumar will buy them back).

1.15pm Alan Jones rang CTB to check on 'who signs cheques?' Told to carry on as normal. Directors are in charge.

4pm Pat Lynch of Lyndon Scaffold Limited leaves a message for CTB to ring him. CTB phones five minutes later, assuming that he is owed money by BCFC. In fact Mr Lynch (PL) states that he is a box holder at BCFC, friend of Manager, Players, Directors and he wants to buy the club. CTB cautious not to give impression that L.C.P. are actively marketing yet, due to need to clarify position. PL states that Sam Kumar is 'getting a barrister to look at the ownership of shares'. CTB says he will contact him next week but that he (CTB) has no idea of price and is just liaising because of his background. Mr Mel Stein has expressed interest (See DS for number).

Saturday 7 November (Author's note: That's what it says in the diary)

Bristol City 2 Birmingham City 0
BCFC now 17th (P 15 W 5 D 4 L 6 pts 19)

Sunday 8 November

Article in *Independent on Sunday* 8/11/92 'Birmingham City's Terry Cooper will stand down if a future owner of the club wishes to bring in his own man. Cooper had agreed a new three-year contract with the Kumar brothers, the club's owners whose business went into receivership last week. Rumours suggest a consortium including boxing promoter Paddy Lynch and millionaire Mike McGinnty, a former West Brom director, is interested.'

PL and his partner are now going public.

Monday 9 November
11am Tom Ross of BRMB Radio calls CTB. Keen to speak to someone. 'Birmingham is anxious to know.' CTB says things will be happening over next few days.

11.15am David Hinde of Sports Marketing speaks to CTB and says he represents a consortium which is interested. Told that over next few days things would be clarified.

12.15pm Mr Russel Black (Nightfreight) (speak to Julie) says he is interested (personally not Nightfreight). He's travelling around this week, but speak to Julie.

12.30pm BRMB ring back – Is it true that BCFC is in Receivership. CTB explains that a company, BRS Kumar is in Receivership, that company lists among its assets 84 per cent of Birmingham City. It might similarly own shares in Marks and Spencers or British Telecom – that wouldn't make them bust, nor does it make BCFC bust.

Tuesday 10 November
Reports on Ceefax say that the Wrublewski Brothers, who run the local basketball team, are interested in the club. Article in *The Times* 10/11/92: Brothers may step in at Birmingham. 'Birmingham City may be bought by the millionaire Wrublewski brothers, the owners of the Birmingham Bullets basketball club. The brothers are putting together an international consortium to bid for the first division club, which was put up for sale last week when the business empire of the Kumar brothers, which owned 84 per cent of Birmingham City, went into receivership. Harry Wrublewski, the Bullets' managing director, said that business interests in the United States, Australia and Britain were involved in the bid. A second consortium, including the boxing promoter, Paddy Lynch, and the millionaire Mike

McGinnty, is also interested in buying City. McGinnty said that he was prepared to help in any way he could – "but only when I know what we have to play for the club".'

9.15am Mr David Bundy – Matafin Group Holdings. Interested in buying. Wants all the information we have.

12.00 Peter White from *The Sun* in the Midlands. Can we confirm Jeff Lynn (CTB's error – not mine), the pop star, is interested? No, we've had various enquiries from individuals and groups.

12.05pm Mark Hulme, Manager of the Football Club shop, enquires whether or not he can continue to purchase from Influence International. Told he can.

4pm *Birmingham Post* phone CTB to confirm who has bid for the club. Off the record, half a dozen or so. Is it true that it'll take £700,000 to buy club (as per Charles MacMillan's quote) – CTB cannot comment but emphasises that no timewasters wanted – Men of substance only and no one allowed to look at the books unless it was a serious bid. CTB explained that Receiver has to sell shares for best possible amount for the sake of BCCI and its creditors. Mr Wiseman (previous owner) had only himself to satisfy. Charles MacMillan has thousands of creditors of BCCI, Bank of England, Sheik of Abudabi. Buyer must pay back loans and pay premium.

4.15pm Fax received from M. Nathanson of Penningtons to say he has a client who is interested. CTB rings to confirm receipt.

4.25pm S.D. Swafen faxes the following to BCFC, Mr Kumar in London and Mr Slater:

I was appointed Joint Administrative Receiver of B.R.S. Kumar Brothers Limited ('the Company') on 2 November 1991. Amongst the assets covered by B.C.C.I's charge over the Company are 84 per cent of the ordinary shares in Birmingham City Football Club plc ('the Club') together with a debt due from the club to Kumar Brothers International Limited which we understand amounts to approximately £426,000.

In addition we were appointed by the High Court as Receivers and Managers of International, a company owned and controlled by Messrs S. Kumar, B. Kumar and R. Kumar. This company, we also understand has advanced further monies to the Club, which we understand to be approximately in the sum of £250,000.

Any proposals you have for the settlement of these sums will be appreciated but we stress that it is not our intention to press for immediate settlement. We are actively looking for a buyer for the company's shareholding in the Club and we would expect such a person to make realistic proposals for these sums to be paid. If you are aware of parties who may be interested in acquiring the shares please let me know and I would be grateful for any suggestions you may have that may assist disposing of the shares.

At the present time, we are not insisting on any change to the composition of the Board of the Club and expect that the Board will continue to manage the Club's affairs. We do wish you to take into consideration the following matters:

1. No further monies can be expected to be made available from the Company to International
2. As majority shareholders we wish to have sight of the latest management accounts of the Club, together with copies of the minutes

of the last twelve board meetings and the cash flow forecasts for the next six months

3. We would require notice of any matters being put to a board for discussion and voting
4. We would require a nominated observer to be allowed to attend all board meetings
5. We are not prepared to condone the sale of any of the playing staff and will actively oppose any such proposals
6. We require your confirmation that all the Club's registers, minute books, documents constituting to the Club's properties, books of account and records are in the Club's possession and are kept at the club's registered office.

We look forward to your urgent response to this letter so that further instructions can be given to the General Secretary and Manager of the club to assist us.

Yours faithfully, for and on behalf of B.R.S. Kumar Brothers Limited

S.D. SWADEN F.C.A. Joint Administrative Receiver

Wednesday 11 November

9am Mr Nathanson rings to say that his client was, until recently, a Managing Director of a Premier League Club, who lives in Solihull.

He asks if the price quoted in *The Times* (£1.25m) is accurate. No comment, but CTB states that it will take a substantial amount, yet to be ascertained.

The Times article:

CUT-PRICE BIRMINGHAM

Birmingham City Football Club could be purchased for as little as £1.25 million following the financial collapse last week of the club's owners (Dennis Shaw writes). This figure would cover the cost to the Kumar brothers when they bought 84 per cent of the club's shares, plus debts of approximately £500,000. The receivers, Leonard Curtis and Partners, are looking for £1.25 million, but will sell to the highest bidder. No firm approaches have been made but another prospective purchaser emerged yesterday, Roy Breuhat, a Channel Islands-based millionaire.

Despite this, the Kumars are seeking to retain control, claiming the appointment of the Receiver was illegal...

9.45am Pat Lynch rings CTB. CTB estimates that within seven days the receivers will be in a position to talk to prospective purchasers who can prove their ability to buy. No price has yet been established. Pat Lynch asks, 'Who's looking after the gate money tonight? Ashok usually does and he's not an employee of the Club.' Not our problem, says CTB, but noted.

12.00 D. Swaden wants list of prospective purchasers (below)

Date of Contact	Name	Comments
05/11/92	Pat Lynch	Representing himself, M. McGinnty and John White. Box holder at club, friend of Terry Cooper
05/11/92	Mel Stein	Expressed interest to D. Swaden
09/11/92	David Hinde of Sports Marketing Limited	Says he represents a consortium,

09/11/92	Russel Black	Owns or works for 'Nightfreight' wishes to purchase as an individual
10/11/92	David Bundy	Owner of Metafin Group Holdings, ex-owner of Stafford Rangers FC
10/11/92	M. Nathanson	Representing a client who was 'until recently, M.D. of a Premier League Club. He would be putting a consortium together'. Could be Reg Brierley, ex-Sheff United

Others who have declared an interest in the press but have yet to contact us.

The Wrublewski Brothers (owners of local basketball team)
Roy Breuhat ('A Channel Islands-based Millionaire')
Plan is to contact them and arrange initial meeting

12.30pm CTB phones Alan Jones, the secretary, to say that a response is required to yesterday's fax so that LCP can come down and prepare information for prospective purchasers. Mr Jones states that the Kumar Bros. are not there and he doesn't know if they are attending the match v Bari tonight. CTB asks him to ensure that the Directors respond.

2.35pm Directors respond as per fax below:

> On behalf of the Chairman of Birmingham City Football Club, I would acknowledge receipt of your letter of the 10th November 1992.
>
> I am instructed to inform you that the matter is in the hands of legal advisers who I assume will contact you in the near future.
>
> Yours faithfully
> Alan G Jones Secretary

4.04pm Harry Wrublewski telephones CTB wants a meeting. CTB states that within 48 hours LCP hope to arrange meetings with interested parties.

That evening Birmingham 1 Bari 1

Thursday 12 November
10am Mr Nathanson rings to say his client is Mr Brian Rowe (ex-QPR Director). He wants to contact Roy Breuhat. CTB phones the *Birmingham Post* to see if they have a number for Mr Breuhat, CTB puts Mr Swain directly in touch with Nathanson.

12.45pm DS requests CTB to contact Alan Jones to check on availability of accountancy information. Mr Slater has said that the letter from the club of 11th was not intended to be confrontational (but rather it was penned by Mr Wiseman as a holding action). Board will be meeting in seven days. CTB asks him to let us know. CTB speaks to Alan Jones he doesn't keep the books, Marion Willmott does. Auditors are Walter J Edwards.

1pm Touche Ross, London suggest that CM makes contact with Gerry Boone of the Manchester office – he's their Football Club expert.

2.05pm CTB rings David Webb at Walter J Edwards. He's in a meeting but his assistant will ask him to call back.

2.06pm CTB rings Gerry Boone – he's in a meeting, will call back.

5pm Chris Moore of Parnell Kerr Forster rings. He has a client who is interested in the club.

5.05pm Fax received from B'ham to say there is a Board Meeting at 4pm nest Thursday (19th), DS says this is late as information required for purchasers. He will ring Slater tomorrow and ask for earlier access.

Friday 13 November
10am: Gerry Boone, partner at Touche Ross, returns CTB's call. He believes that he will sell the club on Receiver's behalf. CTB says he does not involve himself with such discussions but an appointment is made for Monday at 4pm, with CTB, GB and D. Swaden.

12.00 DS speaks to Mr Slater about management information requested. He has no objections to the secretary getting it together and to DS attending the Board meeting.

Sunday 15 November
Reading 1 Birmingham 0 FA Cup

Monday 16 November
10am DS rings CTB to say meeting with Gerry Boone should be postponed as the Kumars were making an offer to take everything back including the club. CTB duly cancels the meeting.

12 DS rings CTB to say meeting is back on, if possible, as the Kumars' offer is embryonic and we'll have to move on with meeting potential purchasers. CTB rings Gerry Boone's secretary.

12.45pm: Alan Jones faxes over agenda for Thursday's Board Meeting:
1. Minutes of previous meeting
2. Matters arising
3. 1992 Accounts
4. Anglo-Italian Tournament (Mr J F Wiseman)
5. Walsall League Meeting (Club secretary)
6. Manager's Report
7. Safety Report
8. Ground Improvement Report
9. BCFC Soccer Shop
10. Any Other Business

17 November 1992
9am CTB contacted by Ashok of Kumar Bros., the financial controller of BCFC. He suggests that a deal is being put together for the brothers to buy everything back, including BCFC. CTB suggest that we are aware of this and we are

moving very slowly, but we must do something, or be seen to be doing something. Ashok agrees and CTB will fax him tomorrow to give him a list of the required information.

11.30am CTB receives fax from London office saying the following are interested, Simon Gidney of Gidney Securities plus Sydney Mitchell Solicitors on behalf of Solihull Borough Amateur and Athletic Club Limited. They have sold their ground and are ground sharing at the moment. They will probably relocate in February, but they wish to be kept informed. Mr R. P. Holland is the partner dealing with it.

3.55pm A. Robertson of Clement Keys. His client Mr Breuhat is interested.

4pm Meeting between DS, CTB and Gerry Boone of Touche Ross. It is agreed that GB will provide a letter outlining his advice on the marketing of the club. He recommends a *Financial Times* advert (to cover the ARs back) and a minimal brochure. (CTB suggests that there could be thousands of applicants). Touche Ross will establish value, deal with shortlisting purchasers, contact FA, Football League etc to let them know what's happening. The manager dealing with it at Touche Ross is Arup Shah.

Wednesday 18 November
10am CTB makes contact with Arup Shah (AS) and asks what information he'll require. CTB undertakes to clear the way with Ashok of Kumars, to provide the info. AS is briefing himself and will come back this pm.

2.20pm Alan Jones seeks CTB to extend loans of Speedie & Sealey. CTB says this is normal trading and up to the Board.

Thursday 19 November
AS rings CTB and says he requires various items of information. He will fax it to CTB to fax to Ashok and BCFC.

Two new prospective purchasers – by phone Derek Bailey of Bailey Packaging Limited and by letter Betterware plc (Andrew Cohen/ Stanley Cohen) CTB rings at 12.05pm to confirm receipt.

Friday 20 November

A day of much activity. *The Times* runs an article: 'Birmingham City have agreed to sell the midfield player, Mark Cooper, son of the manager, Terry Cooper to Fulham for £40,000.'

The Birmingham evening papers yesterday and the national dailies today mention that Terry Cooper has done a deal to sell his son to Fulham. The Receivers had stated in their letter of 10/11/92 that they would not permit the sale of any player. Alan Jones had been told, however, that if an offer came in for a player it should be referred to the Receivers. In this case, the manager pre-empted things by a) receiving an offer b) taking his son to Fulham to agree personal terms c) getting the secretary to draft the appropriate contracts. At 9.30am he (TC) rang CTB to say that if the deal couldn't go ahead, he would have to review his position. CTB discussed matter with Alan Jones and it was agreed that BCFC should gain Chairman's approval, Chairman should clear it with Receivers.

10.30am CTB phoned Samesh Kumar (the Chairman) who is 'in hiding' at Kumars Manchester. He had not been contacted about the proposed sale (although, like CTB, he was being sought yesterday by the Club to let him know what was happening, but could not be found! Nor could CTB!!) until this morning.

He thought it was a good deal. CTB asked him to confirm that he was seeking the shareholders' blessing for it – of course he was. The whole matter was therefore settled. Mr Cooper had run the show from the start to finish. The letter below is despatched to the club in time for the 12noon deadline:

> We refer to our telephone conversation with the Club's manager, Mr Cooper, this morning. We understand that:
>
> 1. An offer has been received for Mr Cooper's son, a member of the playing staff, in the sum of £40,000.
>
> 2. We understand that such an offer is acceptable to the Club and has been approved by the Chairman in accordance with the Club's rules.
>
> We are pleased to confirm that the proposed sale is acceptable to the majority shareholders subject to the consideration being received by the Club in accordance with Football League regulation.
>
> Yours faithfully, for and on behalf of B.R.S. Kumar Bros. Limited
>
> C.Macmillan F.C.S. Joint Administrative Receiver

10.30am The following information has been requested by Touche Ross and CTB faxed it to Ashok at Kumars, London, who stated he will deal with it:

Information Requirements
Re: Birmingham City Football Club
1. Audited statutory account for the three years to 31st July 1990
2. Draft audited accounts or unaudited accounts for the year ended 31 July 1992
3. Budgets and/or forecasts for the year ended 31 July 1992 and any available for subsequent periods
4. Management accounts for the period since 1 August 1992

5. A detailed breakdown of turnover (e.g. match receipts, catering etc.) since 1 August 1987. Recent marketing with details of response

6. Details of attendance trends over the past five years. If available, comparisons of such trends with local competitors (e.g. Aston Villa, West Bromwich Albion). Details of season ticket holders and trends

7. Details of memberships of supporters club. Trends of membership over last five years. Ongoing corporate client details

8. History of the club, particularly concentrating on recent years e.g. promotion to first division last season, but also providing information of formation, early history etc.

9. A copy of the club handbook for the current year

10. Copies of recent football programmes

11. Detail of current playing staff including: age – career history – salaries and bonuses – recent purchases and sales including details of any options, deferred terms etc. – any offers received for players – any recent valuations of the squad. If an independent valuation has been performed, a directors' valuation would be useful – policy towards youth teams. Details of performance of youth and reserve teams in recent seasons

12. Details of recent valuations of the stadium. Are there any capital commitments? Estimates of potential costs due to Taylor Report. Details of recent ground improvement and expenditure. A map of the site and a copy of the boundaries per title deeds

13. Details of trading in shares in Birmingham City in recent years with information of prices paid. Details of any offers received for the club and/or shares in recent years

14. Copies of Articles and Memorandum of Association

15. Details of the 16% minority interest

16. Details of senior club personnel (both administration and team related) including age, career details,

salaries, employment contract and termination details. Organisation structure

17. Pension arrangements
18. Tax details
19. Details of any other trading activities
20. Details of other recent reports or studies carried out by the club

Please note that items to (14) are required by both Touche Ross London and Manchester to perform the valuation and commence on the selling memorandum respectively.

Ashok says we will have it by Monday, if the information is available.

Monday 23 November

Saturday's result: Barnsley 1 Birmingham City 0

9.15am The Birmingham press are on about the visit of DS & CTB to the club this afternoon. The reason for the visit is of interest and CTB explains it is to let the Club know what's going on and to clarify the position with regards to buying and selling players.

12.15pm Arup Shah from Touche Ross hand delivers a letter outlining TR's plans for the sale. There is a problem in as much as the information required is not readily available. CTB telephones Ashok to find out where the information is – Ashok says it will take time, he's not at the club until Wednesday. CTB insists that this is too late and he should provide it earlier. Ashok says he will get what he can immediately. CTB is convinced he is stalling waiting for a deal.

4.30pm Meeting is held at Birmingham's ground. Present: D. Swaden, CTB (- Leonard Curtis) , J. Wiseman, T. Cooper and A. Jones (- BCFC). Major points raised: By Mr Wiseman 1) He'd requested an audit from the Chairman but Ashok said Leonard Curtis did not want one (Not So stated

DS) 2) Midland Bank account operates only one signatory i.e. Samesh Kumar, the Chairman 3) He has had sixteen meetings concerning the Taylor Report. As he understood it, the Football Trust would grant £2m towards a programme costing £3.6m. It was important to get things moving and a consultant needed to be paid £15,000 to get drawings underway. DS says this should be dealt with at Board level urgently; By Alan Jones 1) No home games until December 5 what was the effect on cashflow? No one knows – nor do DS or CTB 2) How long will the timescale be? – 3 months to a sale: By T. Cooper 1) Could he buy/sell players? DS stated we must look at each individual case 2) Any chance of shirts for the club shop. DS established that these were being withheld by Kumar International due to poor payment record of BCFC. The meeting closed at 6pm. A good meeting in everyone's judgement.

Monday 30 November
Saturday's result: West Ham 2 Birmingham City 1
This week, the Judge is due to decide on the fate of International. At that stage the future of the Kumar Bros. will be clearer and, consequently, so will Birmingham.

Tuesday 1 December
The team and supporters fly off to Italy to play against Cesena on Wednesday. Mr Wiseman says there will be a net cost to the club of £5,000 but initially it is having to contract for £39,000 (for the plane) and £20,000 for hotels. The club is selling places and spaces to supporters and the press.

Wednesday 2 December
Judge will decide tomorrow. Meeting arranged with Touche Ross for tomorrow to plan next stage of sale.

Thursday 3 December

Last night: Cesena 1 Birmingham 2

Meeting with Touche Ross. Advert finalised, brochure approved.

2pm News that Judge decided Receivers can stay in at International, but not sell it off until Kumars have had a chance to deal with the Bank. Charles Macmillan tells BBC TV Midlands that an advert will go in the *FT* on Tuesday next.

Ian Atkins, Assistant Manager, is off to Cambridge United.

Friday 4 December

A letter is faxed to the Kumar Bros solicitors by D. Swaden requesting that they resign. DS arranges to go down to BCFC on Monday to request Alan Jones to go on the Board to explain about the advert.

Monday 7 December

DS attends press conference. Good reception

Saturday's result: Blues 1 Brentford 3

Board meeting arranged for Thursday.

Thursday 8 December

Advert appears in the *Financial Times* stating:

LEONARD CURTIS

By order of the joint administrative receivers
Charles Macmillan FCA & Stephen Swaden FCA

In the matter of
BRS KUMAR BROTHERS LIMITED

Offers are invited for 84.23% of the Ordinary shares in
BIRMINGHAM CITY FOOTBALL CLUB

- Professional Football Club in the Barclays League First Division
- Freehold stadium with 27,000 capacity
- Distinguished history: formed in 1875
- 'Big City' location, being a prime catchment area for support
- Annual turnover of approximately £2m
- Significant improvement in recent financial performance
- Real potential for future playing and financial success
- All enquiries should be addressed to Colin Burke at:

Leonard Curtis & Partners, Chartered Accountants
Peter House, Oxford Street, Manchester M1 5AB
Tel: (061) 236 1955 Fax: (061) 228 1929

In *The Times* that day the following article was printed:

Bids invited for Birmingham by Dennis Shaw

Birmingham City FC is today officially advertised as up for sale with offers invited for the 84 per cent shareholding belonging to the Kumar Brothers, its former owners. The shares, understood to be worth around £750,000, went into receivership as a result of the collapse of BCCI, with whom the Kumars had extensive dealings.

Although numerous direct and indirect enquiries have been received already by Leonard Curtis and partners, the firm of accountants handling the sale, no negotiations have yet been undertaken.

Indications are that a controlling interest in the club can be purchased for as little as £1.25 million, although a figure several times that amount would be required to run the club satisfactorily.

Substantial sums need to be spent to bring St Andrew's fully into line with the requirements of the Taylor Report while Terry Cooper, the manager, needs money to revitalise a team which is slipping towards the relegation zone.

Until the shares are sold, the Kumars nominally remain on the board, although effectively Jack Wiseman and Cooper, who is a director, remain until the controlling interest has been purchased. A £5,000 deposit will be required to establish 'genuine' interest in purchasing the first division club.

4pm Mr Stephen Phillips, The Takeover Panel, London rings CTB to point out that BCFC is a plc and the sale of the shares comes within the rules of The Takeover Panel i.e. whoever buys the 84.23 per cent must be for the balance, and the minority shareholders must be provided with sufficient financial information to enable them to make a decision whether or not to accept the offer. Touche Ross are informed – they are already amending the brochure on the advice of their own experts.

Wednesday 9 December
Last night's result: Blues 1 Ascoli 1. Crowd 3,963
Blues now need to win away next week with Brentford losing at home.

Monday 14 December
Saturday's result: Derby 3 Blues 1
This week's schedule:
Brochures to go out – Monday/Tuesday
Blues play in Italy – Wednesday
Board Meeting – Thursday

Kumars have yet to resign – DS will table EGM motion at Board Meeting to dismiss them should they not resign by Thursday.

Tuesday 15 December
Brochures not yet ready from Touche Ross

Wednesday 16 December
Brochures go out

Thursday 17 December
Yesterday's result: Lucchese 3 Blues 0 Crowd 139

Monday 21 December
Saturday's result: Blues 2 Watford 2

CTB attended the meeting. Kumars have still not resigned.

Tuesday 22 December
The first of the positive responses, offering £5,000 deposit is received. The Kumars have still not resigned.

Wednesday 23 December
Charles Macmillan serves formal notice on the club to convene a meeting to sack the Kumars from the Board. Alan Jones organises the formal papers and proxies etc. CTB suggests that, before having to send out 900 notices, after which, no doubt, the brothers will resign and then another 900 notices will have to be sent out to cancel the meeting, Alan Jones should announce that he is convening a meeting to the press.

As a result of that pressure, the brothers may resign before the meeting is called.

Tuesday 29 December

Saturday's game v Sunderland was postponed (with the resulting effect on cash flow). All the other teams at the bottom won and so the Blues are now bottom, with games in hand. They had a match arranged for this evening v Swindon Town, but this has also been postponed.

A Board Meeting was held on Saturday, 26 December and Mr Wiseman was voted into the chair. This has sorted the Bank Mandate out but not the overdraft.

Thursday 31 December

Three definite and two possible expressions of interest moving to the next phase are received by LCP by the deadline.

The 'definites' are:

International Sports & Leisure (Peter Spencer)
Lyndon Scaffolding (Pat Lynch)
Solihull Borough AFC Limited

Two possibles are:

Marshall James and Co representing a client in Toron to and Roldvale Limited (D. Sullivan) saying he'd be prepared to pay £5/600,000 but not £1.4m (who mentioned £1.4m?).

The following persons were contacted to ensure that their applications have not been lost in the post:

Russel Black of Nightfreight – still on holiday, secretary not available, message left to ring back.

David Bundy, Metafin Group Holdings – my accountant will be in touch in next few days with a bid.

Mr Nathanson of Penningtons – his client, Mr Rowe, had been speaking to Mr Breuhat. He would contact him and come back to LCP if any further interest.

Chris Moore, Pannel, Kerr Foster – not at his desk, message left to call CTB.

Harry Wrublewski – not interested in taking it any further.

Mr Brown (Haven Investments) – no reply from number.

Mr Bruehat – withdrawn letter on way.

Betterware plc – no longer interested.

Derek Bailey – no longer interested.

5 January

Confidentiality agreements are sent to; Solihull Borough AFC Ltd, Lyndon Scaffolding plc and International Sports & Leisure Ltd. Notices have gone out convening the AGM to get the Kumars off the Board.

6 January

2pm CTB receives phone calls from a Mr Irving Brown from New Jersey. Claims he met CTB at Man City once. Ex-Salford man who is interested in football and has tried to buy a club in the past. CTB faxes copy of sales pack.

4.35pm CTB receives phone call from Ron Noades, Chairman of Crystal Palace. He has a 'relative' who is interested. CTB sends him a pack to his home address.

7 January

3pm Irving Brown rings again. He is sending off the £5,000 in dollars, can CTB open a dollar account because £1 is going through the floor.

Monday 11 January

Over the weekend Mr Brown has gone public. More important the Blues have won at last!

> *The Times* reports: 'Birmingham City, 2-1 winners at home to Luton Town, but seeking a new owner, have aroused the interest of an American

millionaire. Irving Brown, 53, owns a series of shopping malls in New Jersey and made a bid to take over the club four years ago.'

Cashflow forecasts produced by the club's auditors show a cash requirement of £830,000 by first week in February. This is £130,000 in excess of the limits laid down by Midland Bank and DS approaches BCCI liquidators to provide £100,000 overdraft, to add to the £700,000 from the Midland (the main reason for the excessive borrowing was the postponement of a couple of matches over Christmas due to weather, and the £15,000 payment to the Commercial Manager).

Wednesday 13 January
Brian Rowe, ex-QPR executive, approaches CTB for Irving Brown's telephone number.

Last night's result: Swindon 0 Birmingham 0

Monday 18 January
Yesterday's (Sunday) result: Wolves 2 Blues 1

Closing date for deposits has passed and only three have been received from Lyndon Scaffolding, Solihull Borough AFC and Irving Brown. Additionally, Triton plc have signed a confidentiality document.

Three other parties have suggested they would be keen to follow up their initial interest & CTB phones them:

Marshall James & Co – message left for Mr Brian Marshall to ring CTB.

International Sports & Leisure – message left on ansaphone for Peter Spencer to ring CTB.

Gidney Securities – not interested in any more information – may just make an offer.

Monday 25 January

Confidential memorandum sent out last Wednesday

Last Friday's result: Blues 2 Peterborough 0

Meeting scheduled today to remove Kumars as Directors.

Simon Gidney, Gidney Securities, makes contact with CTB. Could he arrange an informal meeting – Peter House Wednesday 2.30pm.

Lesley Kay of Lyndon Scaffolding contacts CTB before a meeting is arranged – he is sending a list of information requirements.

Tuesday 26 January

The Times reports: Samesh Kumar was voted out of office as chairman of Birmingham City by shareholders at an extraordinary general meeting of the club yesterday. Jack Wiseman will serve as acting chairman until new owners are installed.

Wednesday 27 January

The Sun has an 'exclusive' back page story that Graeme Souness is set to buy the Blues. Terry Cooper rings CTB at 10.10am to say he was not the source. He did, in fact, speak to Souness about buying the Club 12 months ago, but has not spoken to him during the current episode. C. Macmillan issues a press statement neither confirming nor denying.

Thursday 28 January

Last night's result: Southend 4 Blues 0

Saturday 30 January

Blues 0 Cambridge 2

Saturday 6 February

Notts County 3 Blues 1

Tuesday 9 February
Blues 0 Millwall 0

22 February 1993
As a result of a 1-1 draw away to Grimsby on Saturday last (20th), the Blues are propping up the rest of the division. The main parties still involved are:

Paddy Lynch, Peter Stokes and John White – 'The Lynch Mob'.

Roldvale – owned by David Sullivan of *Sunday Sport* fame.

Simon Gidney of Gidney Securities (incorporating Admiral).

Irving Brown of New Jersey.

(Both Triton and Solihull Borough have withdrawn their initial interest, although we have had no formal word from Solihull.)

The diary of Colin Burke continues in the next chapter.

4

Roldvale Buys
The Blues

Mike Wiseman recalls:

'The Receivers of the Kumars' business took a keen interest in the running of the club as the 84 per cent stake in Blues was a major asset which they hoped to dispose of for a good price. Colin Burke, their dedicated insolvency practitioner, was very helpful, and even secured extra borrowing facilities for the club secured on property owned by the Kumars' business. This gave us invaluable time to sort out the club's affairs so that we could actually provide potential purchasers of BCFC reliable and accurate information.

'There was considerable interest in the Blues but a deal needed to be done as the club were sliding towards relegation. Things then happened very quickly after Karren Brady and a property consultant Eamonn Connolly arrived at St Andrew's to inspect the facilities and discuss a possible purchase of the club with Jack. It turned out that they were acting on behalf of David Sullivan and true to form he made an offer for the Blues straightaway, giving the Receivers a week to make their minds up before he withdrew his bid.

'The deal was done within the timeframe requested and Karren was installed in Birmingham to run the club – one of her first actions was to ask Jack whether he would be willing to continue as chairman which he was naturally delighted to do plus he proved to be a great asset to the new regime with his knowledge of the club plus his Football Association connections.'

Colin Burke recalls:

'As I was the case manager, I kept a day-by-day log book of everything that went on. This is in the possession of Keith and certain entries are featured elsewhere in this book. Reflecting back on it after all these years, a few things stand out:

a. Following on from an advert in the *Financial Times* and a subsequent interview I gave to *The Times*, a figure of £1.2m was mooted as the asking price. Within days, David Sullivan had come on and, appreciating that it would be some time until any deal could be completed, said that he'd done his valuation and when I was ready he'd give me £600k for the shares – not a bad estimate, because five months later that's exactly the price he paid. On reflection, I should have just taken his offer on day one, except, of course, that the Stock Exchange rules wouldn't let me.

b. Interestingly, when I first spoke with Mr Sullivan he asked me a very direct question, "Are you a chartered accountant?" When I replied in the negative he replied, "Okay, I'll talk to you as I don't like dealing with chartered accountants!"

c. I was acutely aware that David Sullivan was engaged in a type of publishing which some people would describe as "racy". My concern over this was not a moral one, but rather I suspected that, in the months leading up to any sale, competing potential purchasers would try and blacken his reputation to frustrate his interest. I could well imagine the press headlines and anti-Sullivan campaign that could easily have been launched (a subsequent newspaper headline of "Bumingham Titty" the day after the sale proved my concern to be valid). In the face of a potentially vitriolic public campaign, I could envisage him walking away from the whole thing before we had a chance to finalise a deal. Knowing how wealthy he was, I was convinced he would outbid anyone else and I have to admit to being desperate to get such a real money-man to take over the club and significantly invest in it – but I was equally desperate to keep his involvement a secret, so only a very few individuals at Lennies and Deloittes were in on the knowledge. All I shared with the Wisemans and Alan Jones was that they had to trust me and believe that I was close to securing a deal with an individual buyer whose name I couldn't reveal but who had the financial wherewithal to develop the stadium and the team. My daily discussions with the local press were, I like to think, always informative, but I was constantly careful not to reveal Mr Sullivan's interest. Amazingly for anything to do with football, the secret was kept until the deal was done and the Blues had billionaires as owners! How good was that ? And, in retrospect, I consider that keeping the secret for five months, thus securing the future of the club, to be my greatest achievement in the whole process.

d. During the five months we had scores of expressions of interest and sent sales packs to over 70 people or institutions. Understandably, everybody was trying to pick the shares up as cheaply as they could, but my log book records that I was amused at one particular offer. A Mr Pat Lynch was so keen to do a deal that he convened and attended a meeting with me in Manchester on Thursday 18 February 1992, together with his own accountant, Leslie Kaye and his external advisor, Alistair James of KPMG (Birmingham). Surely, thought I, this was going to be a substantial, perhaps unbeatable offer. The three besuited men came into the boardroom and sat down on one side of the long table, with three of us from Lennies sat opposite them. Everybody was quietly staring at their papers while coffee was served and then, after a long-winded introduction, Mr Lynch made his offer, "We don't think the shares are worth anything – we'll give you £1." At such an anti-climax the room fell silent; after all the preparation and fuss and bother, how does one respond to such an offer? After half a minute I broke the silence when I said, "Come on lads, the coffee cost us £3." They were not amused and the meeting broke up shortly thereafter – and I knew I still had a £600k offer in my pocket.

e. The log also records that a certain Keith Dixon of Triton plc also attended a meeting in Manchester around the same time and announced his plans to sell St Andrew's and move the club to its training ground in Damson Lane and develop it in a similar way to how Walsall developed the Bescot Stadium. He asked me if that would be acceptable. My reply was a simple one; once you have done the deal you can do what you like. It is true to say that I could if the price was right have sold the ground for development and potentially raised more funds for BCCI but it was generally accepted that nobody wanted that to happen. Mr Dixon advised that he would let me know if he intended to proceed.'

Colin Burke's diary continues:

Roldvale have enquired about virtually every aspect of the club and are thinking about an offer. They initially suggested £500/£600k.
Simon Gidney attended Peter House today to offer £15,000 x 36 monthly payments to pay off the inter-company loan and £1 for all the shares. Not bad for a first confirmed bid (£540k – spread).
Irving Brown is awaiting copies of the accounts, after which he will consider making a bid.

4.30pm Roldvale telephone and want to know 'how much?' CTB says DS must make that move. DS agrees to telephone

Roldvale tomorrow having heard from David Webb that the inter-company is £660k.

Tuesday 23 February
DS talks to Roldvale. They offer £750k-800k and want to put people in to have discussions with staff. DS tells them he wants £1m and will talk to them again tomorrow.

Wednesday 24 February
DS confirms with Roldvale that they can send two people down to St Andrew's to meet with the staff and view the place. CTB will meet them there at 3pm Friday.

Thursday 25 February
Irving Brown faxes CTB to say that he is no longer interested. CTB learns from the B'ham press that Brown has joined the Lynch mob.

Friday 26 February
Eamonn Connolly and Karren Brady, representing Roldvale, visit the club with CTB. They meet the staff and tour the ground. They seem keen.

Monday 1 March
Management accounts to 31st Dec 1992 with comparatives for year to 31st July 1992 will be ready by 5.00pm.

The press are keen to trace Karren Brady. They are investigating every avenue to find out her principal. The *Evening Mail* suggests it's Len Walker. CTB cannot comment, says 'it's an investment company and we don't know who'.

Accounts arrive and will be faxed first thing on Tuesday.

Tuesday 2 March
Accounts are faxed to Roldvale and to Lyndon Scaffolding.

11.30am Andy Colquhoun of the *Birmingham Post* rings CTB. 'I'm going to mention a name to you. There is a Karren Brady that works for David Sullivan.' 'Who?' 'David Sullivan of the *Sunday Sport*.' 'Oh him.' 'Well.' 'No, I've not come across his name in this, we're dealing with an investment trust.'

CTB phones Karren Brady, who has already been contacted by the *Post* as has David Sullivan. They have denied any involvement (although she did not actually talk to them). Last year, she and David Sullivan had lunch with the MD of the *Post* and *Mail* (!).

KB says Roldvale will make its bid, lasting for 48 hours, this afternoon.

Wednesday 3 March
No bid received yesterday. Expected today.

Birmingham Post run a story that Karren Brady, a top executive with Sport Newspapers is 'helping' her father, Terry Brady, who has emerged as the chief rival to Birmingham scaffolder, Paddy Lynch.

Bid received by telephone at 11.30am and by fax at 13.19 hours.

> Dear Colin
>
> Further to our telephone conversation, I can confirm my verbal offer of £600,000 for the 84% share of Birmingham City Football Club, the loan and any outstanding invoices from Kumar Bros Ltd to Birmingham City Football Club. We can sort out what is apportioned to what once the price has been agreed.
>
> This offer of £600,000 made by Roldvale Limited is subject to no material changes in the accounts up to the present date and contract.

We have put a great deal of thought into this offer, which is totally unnegotiable and expires at 12 noon on Friday 5th March 1993.

I look forward to hearing from you but direct telephone number is...

Yours sincerely

Karren Brady

CTB telephones P. Lynch and asks him to submit a bid by letter:

Dear Mr Lynch

Re: Birmingham City Football Club plc

I write further to our recent correspondence concerning the above and your telephone conversation with Colin Burke of this office of today's date. I have now received an offer for the 84.23% shareholding in the company. I have not accepted or rejected this and would invite a bid from you and your colleagues by 12.00 noon tomorrow, 4th March 1993.

You will by now have received all the information which I am able to supply, including management accounts to 31st December 1992, along with comparatives detailing the unaudited figures for the year to 31st July 1992. I appreciate that the audited accounts are not yet ready for signature but understand that they will be ready for Friday 5th March. I am prepared to accept an offer which will be subject to there being no significant differences between the unaudited figures and the audited accounts.

You will of course be aware that I cannot offer any warranties or indemnities in this sale.

I look forward to hearing from you in the near future

Yours faithfully, for BRS Kumar Brothers Limited

C.Macmillan F.C.A. Joint Administrative Receiver

CTB faxes Simon Gidney to phone CTB. Simon Gidney says he will bid by 12 noon tomorrow. He's in discussions with an 'Italian Conglomerate'.

The *Birmingham Post* are now convinced D. Sullivan is behind Karren Brady.

Thursday 4 March
By midday, Simon Gidney has made his offer of £600,000 over 'three or four years'.

CTB faxes DS and CM

At 12.17pm today I received a telephone call from Simon Gidney stating that he is not in a position to make an offer today but he will be on Monday if we have not sold the shares beforehand. His offer will be £600,000 over a three to four year period and he would be looking to complete the deal by Friday 12th March.

The payment would be in the form of monthly instalments and he believes he has sufficient information to obviate the need for a confidential sales pack.

That only leaves the Lynch Mob.

Irving Brown has flown over from the USA and is meeting them all at the Hyatt Hotel in Birmingham to come up with a deal.

2.45pm Irving Brown rings CTB. Is it true, he asks, that they will have to come up with £750,000 to beat Sullivan?

That's not far out, but make a bid at the level you can support. 'That's way out of our league because we want the money to go into the club.'

4.33pm Lyndon Scaffolding, the Lynch Mob's vehicle concedes by fax:

> Thank you for your effort in obtaining the further information requested.
>
> I write to confirm the telephone conversation between Irving Brown and yourselves this afternoon.
>
> We remain very keen to make a realistic offer should any problems arise in your current negotiations.
>
> Yours faithfully
>
> L.J.Kaye F.C.A. for and on behalf of P.A.Lynch & Partners

Friday 5 March

9am Roldvale are informed that their bid has been accepted as long as the deal can be done straight away, the suggestion being that a higher bid has been received and it involves stage payments. Both lawyers are instructed to 'get it done by two o'clock'.

By 1.30pm deadlock looks to be on the cards. Mr Sullivan wants to pay by cheque. If he does so, C. Macmillan will not complete until it clears. If he cannot complete today, he doesn't want it (a threat he makes lightly). 'But seriously, he says, I'm desperate to complete today. I want to go into that dressing room tomorrow and offer them 10 grand to stay up.' OK says CM, give us a banker's draft. I'll give you one for £590,000, 10 grand discount for cash (his money, he admits, sits on the money market until Mondays, so he doesn't want to lose the interest). No deal.

Compromise: we complete today, subject to cheque clearing. Papers will be put in escrow. Sullivan can have his press conference at the club on Saturday and say he's bought it, which he is happy he has, in the knowledge that his cheque will not bounce. CM says 'That's what Maxwell said the day before he went for a swim!' Leonard Curtis will strategically say nothing so that if it goes wrong they will not have to withdraw any statement.

Deal effectively done at 4.20pm.

Saturday 6 March
The plan is

11.30am Board Meeting at which CTB will announce formally the takeover (NB: The Directors have been kept informed informally ahead of the press throughout the last few days and CTB is satisfied that the protocol has been observed).

12 noon Press Conference to be addressed by Sullivan and Brady.

3pm Kick-off against Oxford.

4.45pm Three points.

As if to prove that even God has a sense of theatre, everything goes according to plan and the Blues win 1-0 after Karren Brady and Jack Wiseman go on to the pitch to meet the crowd. The Board has been informed that it should not contract for the company until the cheque has cleared but otherwise, off you go!

It is worth noting that in November 2016, Roldvale Limited, Ramillies House, Ramillies Street, London, W1F 1LN, had a net worth of £1.6m, cash £969,300, assets at £1.4m, and liabilities of £168,800.

In November 2016, Roldvale Trading Limited of the above address had a net worth of £8.8m, cash £1.7m, assets £6.8m, and liabilities of £1.1m.

5

David Gold and David Sullivan

David Sullivan

I only met David Sullivan on a few occasions at games in the early days of Triton's sponsorship of the Blues and only for short periods. David is one of those people with whom you get an instant rapport. Immediately I knew him to be straight-talking, enthusiastic and generous of spirit.

It doesn't happen that often but it did in 2015 when Paul Robinson and I were at the talkSPORT studios in London to promote Paul's biography, *Robbo – Unsung Hero*, on the Hawksbee and Jacobs afternoon show. In the green room I shared a few words with Darren Gough, the cricketer and again I knew instantly that he was a 'good bloke', just like David Sullivan.

David's generosity is brilliantly evidenced in Barry Fry's book *Big Fry*.

Fry writes, 'He inquired about the New Year's Eve arrangements, where we were staying and whether or not I would allow the lads a celebratory drink, and when I told him that we would be at the Swallow Hotel in Waltham Abbey, close to his Essex home, he invited us all round to his place for dinner. "F***ing hell, David," I said. "I'm taking the whole squad. There will be about 28 of us." He just smiled and said that would be fine.

'We went by coach on the short journey to his £7 million mansion and, judging by the expressions on some of the players' faces, you would have thought they had just entered paradise through the imposing iron gateway which swept open to allow us entry. He had arranged for a band playing 60s and 70s music to entertain us through dinner and afterwards he asked if anybody would like to play tenpin bowling. He just happened to have an alley!

'When the players said they would like that, but had no shoes, he opened a few cupboards displaying every size of appropriate footwear and the game commenced to the accompaniment of a jukebox. We were in a different world and everybody had a wonderful evening, rounded off nicely when he allowed each member of the assembled party to make a telephone call to greet their nearest and dearest. If they had not so far been impressed by their chairman, they were now.

'Dave Sullivan is a rich man, who likes to indulge his passion and I was interested to learn that he made his first £500 from selling bundles of football programmes.'

David's honesty is not appreciated by everyone and that would certainly include Simon Jordan, who describes dealing with him in his 2009 book entitled *Be Careful What You Wish For*. He writes, 'Assessing an ownership style comes down to three key factors: motivation, mentality and the way you do business. On the simplest level, Birmingham's three owners – the Gold brothers and Sullivan – are caricatures. Operators, not fans. They used to own part of West Ham, and Sullivan looked at Cardiff, Watford, Bradford, Leeds and Spurs before Birmingham. His ambition is neatly split: half on his Birmingham Village casino plan, and half on leaving. He'd like to own a London club instead "because of the travelling from Essex – I'm fed up with it".

'Second, the mentality. If I see another David Gold interview on the poor East End Jewish boy done good I'll impale myself on one of his dildos. These guys are desperately pleased with themselves, they're in it for the profile and they don't do criticism. In 2001, when a handful of fans reacted to Sullivan sacking Trevor Francis by pasting his face on a poster of Osama Bin Laden with the tagline, "Wanted Dead or Alive – Ivor Bin Sulking – Lives in a bunker somewhere in Essex. Sick of Blues fans, sick of criticism and sick of Trevor Francis", Sullivan reacted like this, "I'm fed up with them slaughtering me... I can do without the grief." He tried to sell, couldn't find a buyer and five years later he's still there.

'Third – their business ethic. I've had enough dealings with them to fill the paper, but here's the most recent. Before our game against Birmingham last season, Sullivan came over to me and said, "Simon my boy, Simon – we know what you lot are like with bad decisions, we don't want any bad decisions" – referring to Andy Johnson's spurious "diving" image. So 12 months later, imagine my surprise when Sullivan told the press I'd rejected his £6.5m bid for Johnson. There was no bid, no approach, no inquiry, nothing. Sullivan misled the press and his public in an attempt to unsettle my player, and to make himself and Birmingham look ambitious.

'Sullivan would "love to buy West Ham", currently up for sale, but not while he still owns Birmingham. "The fans really want the Sultan of Brunei or someone," Sullivan says. "I've no desire to spend my sons' inheritance on football and we just don't have the money to compete with bigger clubs."'

Colin Burke recalls:

'Over the months I'd developed a good rapport with David Sullivan, although I never actually met him face to face until the press conference at which the sale was announced. I believe that he trusted me and I certainly trusted him. So I was deeply concerned when, in the meeting of my superiors held to confirm that his was the highest and therefore accepted offer, someone suggested that I go back to him and tell him that, at the 11th hour, we'd had a higher bid, on the presumption that this would cause him to up his price. "Have we had one?" I remember asking. "No, but tell him we have," came my instruction.

'Well you can imagine how reluctant I was to carry out that order. After five months of straight talking and honest dealing, Mr Sullivan and I had reached what was a great conclusion for all parties; now I was being asked to try and "con" him, and the idea did not sit easy with me. Some people may say "that's business, and the art of negotiation", but I saw it as a breach of trust. After a few minutes' consideration back at my desk, I made the call, "Good morning David, Colin Burke here. Listen, I've been told to tell you that we have a higher offer."

'There was a moment's silence at the other end and then he replied, "Okay, Colin. Well go back and tell them that I withdraw my offer. And they can come back to me in a week, by which time it'll be reduced to £400k. And if they come back to me in a fortnight, it'll be £200k." Perfect! I passed the message on and, as they say, the rest is history. On reflection, perhaps I understand now why David Sullivan didn't like dealing with chartered accountants!'

James Nursey of the *Daily Mirror* wrote an article printed on 29 October 2007:

DAVID GOLD AND DAVID SULLIVAN

Birmingham's controversial outgoing chief David Sullivan reckons he has been driven out of St Andrew's by ungrateful fans. And he has warned incoming owner Carson Yeung that running the club should come with a health warning.

Sullivan, 60, is due to collect around £25million next week for selling his shares in Yeung's £80m takeover. But it has come at a cost as the tycoon reckons his stressful reign at City has made him ill on occasions. Sullivan feels taken for granted by Brum fans despite leaving City in the Premier League after inheriting a team doomed to relegation to the third tier. And he insists he had no option but to eventually sell up to Yeung, who first tried to buy City in 2007, 'I will leave heartbroken.

'I have given 16-and-a-half years of blood, sweat and tears. I feel very sad because deep down I feel the supporters decided my time was up and they wanted a change. They rioted 18 months ago when we were relegated at home to Blackburn and there is no other word to describe it. I knew at that moment I had to go – it was just a matter of time. I didn't want to go in the Championship, I wanted to leave the club in the Premier League.'

Publishing magnate Sullivan, worth around £500m, said his farewells to City staff after attending their game at Burnley last weekend. It marked the end of an era after Sullivan, the Gold brothers and Karren Brady all rescued Birmingham from oblivion in 1993. But despite revamping the club on and off the pitch and masterminding promotion last term, Essex-based Sullivan is still unpopular with many fans.

He added: 'I don't think we have got any credit at all from the supporters. I think they will look back in ten years and think they got 16-and-a-half years of very good custodianship. People say we don't spend enough money on players but what people don't see is the money we spend on wages.

'We had the highest wage bill in the Championship last season. And when you get beaten by Blackpool home and away and you have three players earning more than their entire squad you do feel a bit ill.

'They wiped the floor with us away and it makes you feel ill and physically sick. People think you don't care but it breaks your heart when you have slopped all the way to Blackpool. We lost £12million last year as a club to chase promotion but thankfully we got back up.'

Yeung paid an initial £15m for a 29.9 per cent stake in Birmingham in July 2007 but is now set to control the club. Sullivan said: 'He might do a wonderful job – he has promised us he is going to pump in a lot of money. I think the team is two players short of a good team. They need a tall goal-scoring striker and a midfielder.'

Supporters are already looking forward to the new regime with Yeung planning to expand Birmingham into China.

But Brum's crowds have been poor this season with just 19,922 attending their opening home fixture with Portsmouth following promotion. Sullivan thinks fans have voted with their feet because they have not like his outspoken opinions. He said: 'I think I am too honest.

'When we got a gate of 19,000 for the first game against Portsmouth I said that is not good enough and that is not what people want to hear. I am also not from Birmingham but no one from Birmingham ever wanted to buy the club so it is not like I outbid local people.

'Throughout our stay we have asked for local people to join us and invest in the club but no one ever has. Yet the expectation level is so high and whatever you deliver is not enough.'

Sullivan is leaving feeling unloved but West Ham fans would no doubt be delighted if he bought their club.

David's honesty together with an attitude which is 'I'll say what I want' is reflected in two matters involving high-profile international players. In April 2009, Frenchman Franck Queudrue was voted Birmingham's Player of the Year and David believed he helped him achieve the award. Twelve months prior to that, following relegation from the Premier League, he labelled Franck as 'a pile of rubbish' but the £2m signing from Fulham got the fans' vote to win the coveted trophy.

Sullivan claimed, 'I am sure what I said spurred him on. I am pleased to see he has responded to criticism.'

The second involves former Aston Villa striker Dwight Yorke, who describes in his book *Born to Score* one of the most controversial incidents of his career. It happened when relegation-threatened Blues went to Ewood Park to play Yorke's former club Blackburn Rovers.

He writes, 'But as I was among the substitutes, sitting there engrossed in the game, thinking about what I may be able to do if and when I got on, I became more and more aware of this guy seated near to the dugout racially abusing me. I'm not going to describe the abuse and give it a voice, but I will say that in all my years in England, I had never run into this behaviour before. But it was that lack of respect again – and it got the same response as the thief who thought he could just steal from me.

'A rage swept over me and I found myself confronting this guy and telling him if he didn't shut up I would "take him out" – thankfully a confrontation was avoided when the stewards arrived to march the moron away.

'Unfortunately, that wasn't the end of it. I took great exception to one of the Birmingham owners, David Sullivan, claiming in interviews with the media that I had made too much of this incident. I had never met this guy but I could not believe that he had voiced such an ignorant and insensitive opinion. I was told that I should take no heed of it by Brucey (Steve Bruce), but I was disgusted by his attitude. What the hell did he know about it?'

Sam Allardyce, writing in his book *Big Sam – My Autobiography*, says,

'The Hammers' owners David Gold and David Sullivan worked in tandem with the vice-chair Karren Brady. Steve Bruce, who was manager at Birmingham when they were there, warned me they could be hard to work with, particularly Sullivan who took such a keen interest in the club that he could send his managers up to 30 e-mails a day and expect answers to every one of them.

'Steve's tip was, "Don't answer them or he'll just send even more." However, Steve did say that once a player was identified as a target, Sullivan was good at quickly sorting out the deal.'

DAVID GOLD AND DAVID SULLIVAN

Colin Tattum recalls:

'David Sullivan, as I have mentioned, was a character who, in my experience, never told a lie. He would always answer honestly and on some occasions he was too honest and I had to tell him we couldn't actually use some of the things he gave his opinions on. He never fudged an issue whether it was to do with players or their wages. He would always take my calls and often gave me privileged information, even if it was off the record. For example, he phoned Harry Redknapp up once when he was in Dubai and offered him the Blues manager's job.

'The relationship between Sullivan and the *Birmingham Mail* was not always harmonious and in the early days Karren Brady tried to sue the paper and accused us of bias. This wasn't true and in turn the newspaper came back with a counter claim of a dozen or so malicious falsehoods that had been spread to shareholders of the company.

'There were a lot of bullying tactics in those first few years and it was a case of standing your ground. But there was never a dull moment to say the least. I was banned by Brady a couple of times and then a few years later invited for an informal interview for the current job I am now in at the club; it just wouldn't have worked at that time, and I think we both knew it.

'And ironically, in one of his last actions before he returned to Hong Kong and Andy Walker left, Peter Pannu banned me. Andy and I just ignored it but, technically, I was still banned when I joined as head of media and communications – can I "un-ban" myself?'

Mike Wiseman recalls:

'David Sullivan was a most interesting man too as he was incredibly hard-working and would expect all his close associates to be available 24/7. I always thought he was at his best in particularly difficult times as he would never panic and always come up with a very logical plan to rescue the situation.

'I will never forget him ringing Jack just before he was due to have major heart surgery to inform him that he had personally deposited £1m into the club's bank account – the club was engaged in the rebuilding of the Tilton Road and Kop Stands and he wanted to assure everyone that any bills could be paid in case he ended up in intensive care for longer than planned.'

David Sullivan and David Gold

Colin Tattum recalls:

'David Gold is a charming, amenable and decent guy who complemented David Sullivan perfectly, they worked well as a pair and he definitely understood the need for a connection with the fans. They were very different in the way they went about their business and their public personas were contrasting. I found them both fair and fine to deal with and although David Sullivan had a penchant for telling it like it was, regardless of the fall out, he was always very honest and up-front and I would like to think both trusted me during the course of our reporter-owner relationship.'

One interesting inside story is that David Sullivan told me that prior to him selling to Yeung that he had seen his bank account and was able to evidence that he had a balance in excess of £100m.

In truth, Sullivan and the Golds couldn't believe how much Yeung was overpaying (about three times the actual value of the shares).

'They had lost motivation and taken their eye off the ball somewhat, especially after the casino stadium plan was sunk, in the couple of seasons to this point. They knew the majority of fans wanted a change and they knew they had to leave. I always say that they did very well for Birmingham City and very well out of Birmingham City.'

David Gold

After the club was sold to Carson Yeung, David Gold, rather naively in my opinion, offered to stay on as chairman even though he had received a large sum of money for his shares from Grandtop International Holdings.

I operate as a non-executive chairman for a number of companies within the UK and in my experience it is extremely rare for the chairman of an acquired company to be retained by the purchaser.

Normally only executive directors who can add value to the business post-acquisition are retained in their pre-acquisition roles. Nevertheless, David made his offer and then went public over his disappointment that Yeung had not responded to his offer to stay on.

BLUES INSIDER

The *Birmingham Mail* reported:

Yeung's £81.5m takeover is set to go through today and Gold has reluctantly accepted that he will be forced to leave Birmingham if the Hong Kong-based businessman has not got in touch with him before this afternoon's anticipated announcement to the Stock Exchange, when the Midlands club are expected to confirm that the offer has been declared unconditional in all respects, heralding the beginning of a new era at St Andrew's.

While David Sullivan, Birmingham's plc chairman, and Karren Brady, the club's managing director, signalled their intention to move on and make a fresh start elsewhere, Gold opted to hold talks with Yeung's representatives, Sammy Yu and Peter Pannu, to discuss remaining in his current role to provide some continuity between the board and Alex McLeish, the manager, and to assist the new regime with getting to grips with the running of the club.

Gold initially sensed that Yu and Pannu were receptive to the idea and felt there was genuine enthusiasm for his suggestion but the lack of communication since has led him to believe he will not be offered the chance to hold on to his position. Indeed, it appears more likely that Yeung will propose that Gold becomes vice-president of the club, a position the 72-year-old would not be interested in accepting as it would dilute his responsibilities.

Either way, Gold is not prepared to play a waiting game and, having heard nothing from

Yeung or his representatives, he is preparing to bring an end to his 16-year tenure at St Andrew's and look for a new opportunity. He is determined to remain involved in football and will consider both investing in a club on his own as well as working alongside Sullivan, his long-term business partner at Birmingham who has been linked with a takeover at West Ham United.

'I want to make it clear that I am not a willing seller, I never have been. Suffice to say, had I not agreed to sell my shares this would still be going ahead and I would be left in no man's land, a bit like Carson Yeung was when he took 29.9 per cent. My brother, Ralph, was not a willing seller either in the past but now he is and we know David Sullivan's views. It's a bit different for me. I've been here 16, almost 17 years, and for the past 12 years as chairman.

'I would like to think that when the change is made the club will have been left in a better state than it was due to our work. And I would sincerely hope I could stay on in some capacity. Not as a nodding dog you see on the back shelf of a car, but in a role whereby I could take an active part in the running of the football club. It has been mooted that they might want to do that but Carson Yeung may bring in his own people. But certainly, even if for a transitional period, I would be happy to stay involved.'

Gold also believes that Yeung would be well advised to retain the services of managing director Karren Brady. He added: 'Whether Karren will stay, nobody knows for sure. But in talks with the Chinese, I have been trying to persuade them to make sure she does. They need someone to keep the ship steady as we move from one era to the next. Carson Yeung and his backers are serious people, but they are without experience of running a Premier League football club.

'I would imagine that with their business sense – these people wouldn't be in this position now if they did not possess decent business acumen – they would have worked that out for themselves, that they need key personnel to stay, if only for a while. I have taken over a number of businesses myself in the past and I know how important it is to keep together key staff to maintain continuity.

'Without that, then it is extremely difficult, and especially in the case of a football club coming into the hands of overseas owners.'

6

Karren Brady

I FIRST met Karren on Tuesday 9 March 1993 at 2.30pm in her office in the old stand at St Andrew's. At the time I was managing director of Triton plc who were the club sponsors for Birmingham City having negotiated a 'value for money' contract with Samesh Kumar.

Karren had called the meeting to discuss the future of the sponsorship deal. After being escorted into her office I was told without any preamble that she was looking to re-negotiate the sponsorship deal on behalf of the new owners, as the current contract was no longer valid.

Her approach was extremely direct which I felt was mainly due to inexperience rather than a tactic on her part. She was obviously hoping that I would accept her position and she seemed surprised when I immediately responded by saying that the contract was with Birmingham City Football Club; that legal entity remained intact after the receivership of the Kumar brothers' business and that any attempt to renege on its conditions would result in legal action. Faced with losing that argument, she immediately criticised me for the state of the away dressing room. (Note: As part of the sponsorship deal we had agreed to refurbish the home dressing room.) She said that the home dressing room was great but the away dressing room was a disgrace. As politely as I could I suggested that she was new to football and if she went to any ground in the country the home dressing room will always be better than the away dressing room as it is part of the 'psychology of the game'. She conceded the second point and the meeting came to an abrupt end. She saw no need for any preamble or normal meeting protocol in those days.

Nothing changes regarding the psychology of the dressing room. Today's home dressing room consists of quality wooden benching with matching overhead storage cupboards, a flat screen television and sound system plus a fully equipped treatment room with four tables and a bath plus toilets/showers and décor to a high standard. Today's away dressing room consists of basic wooden benching and a table plus basic shower and toilets.

She developed a reputation for being a difficult person with which to negotiate as was evidenced when a friend of mine, Jim Beeston OBE, tried to overcome a situation between the club and Railtrack. Jim was CEO of the Birmingham Heartlands Development Corporation from 1992–98 and was therefore sufficiently well-connected to get some senior Railtrack officials to travel to Birmingham to meet with Karren. The meeting was called to try and resolve a dispute which existed over the ownership of a strip of land behind the Railway end.

When I asked Jim how the meeting went he replied that there had been no negotiation. Karren had simply stated her position and as Railtrack could not agree, the meeting closed almost as soon as it had started. Jim felt it would have been easier to negotiate with a terrorist!

Though relegation to the Third Division meant the club was no longer bound by the Taylor Report's 1994 deadline for conversion to an all-seater stadium, David Sullivan continued the £4.5 million development of St Andrew's as planned.

After the last home game of the 1993/94 season, the Kop and Tilton Road terraces were demolished, helped by fans who took home a significant proportion as souvenirs, and the land was cleared – the rubbish tip beneath the Kop which had earned the club £800 in 1906 (£43,300 at 1994 prices) cost £250,000 to decontaminate and by the start of the new season, 7,000 seats in the Tilton Road Stand were ready for use. On completion of the Kop Stand, the stadium was formally re-opened in November 1994 by Baroness Trumpington, representing the Department of National Heritage who unveiled a commemorative plaque and presented a cheque for £2.5 million on behalf of the Football Trust; the ceremony was followed by a friendly match against Aston Villa, attended by a crowd of 20,000. Planning permission for an all-seater Railway Stand was granted in March 1995, but work was delayed by a dispute over land owned by Railtrack and the stand opened only in 1999.

The media loved the comedic opportunity that arose when the club was officially bought by David Sullivan, a sex industry baron and infamous publisher of the Sport newspapers. Would the club be renamed Birmingham Titty, would there be a Page 3 girl in the matchday programme or sex line numbers on the players' shirts? The appointment of Karren as managing director was a bold one from Sullivan, which was always likely to bring about ridicule from the football industry – she was under 30, a woman and a good-looking one at that. There is the story of when Karren first met Doug Ellis, the chairman of Aston Villa and also a previous director of Birmingham City. Doug in his inimitable way apparently kissed her hand (very old school) addressed her as 'darlin' (very politically incorrect even in 1993) and then asked her who she worked for – she replied Birmingham City to which 'Deadly Doug' replied, 'Which department in the city council?'

I expect such macho attitudes helped drive Karren to become the best-known woman in British football who is regularly on our television screens and in our national newspapers. As David Sullivan put it, 'They thought she would be some bimbo, 25-year-old version of Barbara Windsor, but they found she was a smart cookie.'

Karren was the perfect opposite to Sullivan. He was short and podgy, drinking low-calorie orange drinks while those around him in the boardroom bare of trophies get stuck into the pre-match drinks. He is a curiously innocent figure, touched by his warm reception.

Brady on the other hand loved being in the limelight: signing replica shirts for the fans, autographing books, programmes and body parts and even accepting demands for kisses, on the cheek of course.

Karren had become a celebrity overnight, to the extent that at the start of the 1993/94 season, The Sunday Times ran an article in its supplement The Magazine on 22/08/1993 by Thomas Quirke entitled '*The lady swings the Blues*'.

In the article Quirke demonstrates that:

> An old woman touches her hair and pronounces her 'lovely' in a broad Brummie accent. Brady, greeting even the programme sellers by name, buzzes around the ground from a sponsor's reception to the home dressing room. After primly checking that everyone is covered she ushers in two dazzled lads who had written to ask whether they could meet the team as a 21st-birthday treat. They were stunned to be told to join Brady outside, half-an-hour before one of the most important matches in the club's history.
>
> Brady is charm on legs, often encased in a mini-skirt. She is a hands-on manager; everyone

is touched on the arm, and the favoured few get a friendly rub on the back, including the referee, who is also invited to the post-match party. It must, she worries, infringe some rule or other.

She was instantly the one person local radio wanted for pre-match chats, well ahead of the manager at the time Terry Cooper. Even supposed hard case journalists like Central TV's Gary Newbon were eating out of her hand.

Karren never failed to deliver for the sponsors or the fans, as Thomas Quirke related:

As kick-off approaches, Brady marches on to the pitch to present a silver salver to the team's main sponsor, the local firm Triton Showers, and the Spion Kop stand, stamping ground of a supporters' gang called the Zulu Warriors, launches into a spirited anthem: 'One Karren Brady...there's only one Karren Brady...one K-a-r-r-en Bray-a-dy... there's only one Karren Brady.'

I was interviewed by Quirke for his article and I said how grateful I was for Karren's attention to detail because when they took team photos she thoughtfully told the players not to fold their arms, footballer-style, covering up the Triton logo. I also noted that one of the first things she got me to do on behalf of the fans was to improve the state of their toilets which she described as appalling. When I was asked what I thought of The Sport newspaper I was able to reply that I thought it was a quick read and was economical with the truth about how many times I purchased the newspaper.

Initially she was a real ambassador for the fans and immediately addressed their dislike of the 'dolly mixture' strip, which was designed by Samesh Kumar not Triton, reverting to the traditional blue-and-white kit that was universally revered since the days of Trevor Francis.

In her early days she established a reputation for being ruthless, certainly in terms of getting rid of members of staff. Whilst the club was spending over a million pounds on new players, she was sacking all but two members of staff, including the reserve-team coach and the chief scout, Bill Caldwell, who was also head of catering for a time – at the time it was that type of club. Firing people is not something she likes and she has said often that it is the worst part of any job and something that has to be done when there are no alternatives. Her ruthlessness resulted in getting Birmingham City into the 20th century, even stopping the routine of making all employees and players queue up the stairs to the reception area of the office to collect their wages/salaries every Wednesday morning.

Not long into her time at St Andrew's she was required to clarify her relationship with Sullivan as it seemed the entire city believed she was Sullivan's girlfriend. At the time she was quoted as stating in the local press, 'I know everyone thinks I earned this job between the sheets but I'm not bonking him [Sullivan].)

There is no doubt that she admires Sullivan and has supported him when he was rejected by the horse racing fraternity and when his motives for buying Birmingham City were questioned. It is my understanding that Sullivan was a bachelor in his mid-forties, wealthy and looking for amusement – he found that in Birmingham and in the main the city appreciated what he did for the club in the short, medium and long term in terms of financial support. Although she quelled the rumours about an affair with Sullivan the media still wanted more information on her love life. In the *Sunday Times Magazine* article she is quoted:

'I was brought up a Catholic and have had only two serious relationships,' she says, insisting that, contrary to rumours, neither of them was with a well-known black footballer from Arsenal, the team that she and her father follow fervently. She remains single, and when she first arrived in Birmingham there was a predictable and unsuccessful competition among some Villa stars to score with her. Her own players would not dare to try. One, who ventured a sexist remark about her cleavage, was silenced with the response: 'If I sell you to Crewe, you won't be able to see them from there.'

She held strong opinions in those early days – I prefer older men as I can learn from them – footballers are only interested in drinking, clothes and the size of their willies – remember she ultimately married the footballer Paul Peschisolido.

At the time there was a popular Channel 4 drama series called The Manageress and it was inevitable that she would be compared with that role but she was always dogmatic that she knew nothing about football and left all footballing matters to the manager – this lack of footballing knowledge was adequately demonstrated when she mistook Aston Villa's West Indian striker, the late Dalian Atkinson as the son of the then Villa manager, Ron Atkinson.

Her interest in politics was announced early on in her career when she was quoted in the local press: *I could really kick ass in politics.* She certainly achieved her aim, being involved in the Remain campaign in the 2016 referendum on the UK's membership of the European Union and gaining membership of the House of Lords.

With her background she is a Tory blue and her role model must be Margaret Thatcher, who like Karren broke male dominance in her chosen field of influence.

Her true ability is that of public relations. There was the time when Maradona was to join the Blues and would be paid £20,000 to play in a pre-season friendly against Liverpool as a way of assessing his fitness – as they say, no progress. She also promised that St Andrew's would be transformed into an all-seater stadium costing £4.5m – as they say, no progress. Having said that, the pre-season friendly took place and ended in a penalty shoot-out which Blues won and ground improvement expenditure exceeded £200,000. As Colin Tattum said at the time, 'There hasn't been such excitement at St Andrew's since Trevor Francis played here in the mid-70s.'

Arriving to take over the role of managing director of Birmingham City at the age of 23 wearing a short skirt and driving a Porsche was manna from heaven for the local and national press. A publicity stunt which she repeated in 2010 when she joined the popular BBC show The Apprentice, when in the opening credits she arrived at Lord Sugar's offices in a Porsche and shows off the obligatory amount of leg.

She was immediately dubbed 'The First Woman of Football', paving the way for further female appointments to the boards of English football clubs; Delia Smith was appointed as a director of Norwich City in November 1996 and Lorraine Rogers became a non-executive director of Tranmere Rovers in 1998 before taking on the role of executive chairman the following year.

In January 2010, Karren was appointed vice chairman of West Ham United FC. In January 2011, under her leadership campaign, the club moved from Upton Park in Boleyn Road to the Olympic Stadium for the 2016/17 season.

At the time of writing this book I am reading Danny Dyer's book *Life Lessons from the East End* and he is fairly disturbed by the news that West Ham United are making this move. He says:

'West Ham is a proper football club. It's right in the middle of the community, you have to go through streets of terraced house to get there – this ain't some soulless new stadium with plenty of parking and a nice fat A road running up to the door. It feels well urban, tower blocks and houses crowding in against the ground. The roads around it are dirty, full of traffic.' Later he says, 'But I fear for West Ham, I really do.

'We're moving out of the Boleyn Ground – Upton Park – and into the Olympic Stadium. I remember when we had the Chicken Run down the side of the pitch, fans close enough almost to touch the players. Will that be the case in the new stadium? I doubt it! Now we're going to have a running track between us and the pitch? And really, the stadium ain't even in West Ham. It's quite Essexy. I'm scared it'll change the club I love too much, it'll just become another sporting concession or whatever they call them. The future is very uncertain. I hope for the best but I tell ya this – I fear the worst.'

In her 2012 book entitled *Karren Brady – Strong Woman – Ambition, Grit and a Great Pair of Heels,* in chapter 3 she states:

'... thought I was a publicity stunt when I showed up in 1993 at the age of 23 to run a football club. As a woman, my looks and the way I dressed came under a lot of scrutiny... If I was going to be used as a distraction, I would use it to help promote my business. If I had to appear in a football kit to make sure the sponsor paid a fortune and the picture made the front page, so be it.'

Well let's correct that statement, because I was the managing director of the sponsor and we never paid a fortune to the club. However, she gave us lots of free publicity when she did don a Triton kit for the *Sunday Times* feature and also for the front cover of her 1995 book entitled *Brady Plays the Blues – My Diary of the Season.*

On 25 April 2009 Gil Merrick was guest of honour at the home game against Preston North End as the club had decided to rename the Railway End 'The Gil Merrick Stand' for the 2009/10 season. Gil and I had been at a *Gil Merrick* book signing at WH Smith in Solihull in the morning and then collected Gil's wife Ivy and Malcolm Page before going on to have lunch in the Boardroom Club at St Andrew's. This was a major reunion for Gil and the club, as he had not had any relationship with the senior management of the Blues since his sacking on 30 April 1964. So here we were 45 years on and at long last the board of directors had decided to embrace their history. Towards the end of our meal Karren came over to Gil and welcomed him back to the club and she made quite a fuss of him. As she walked away Gil looked over to Malcolm and said, 'Who was that?' Fortunately Karren did not hear him.

It was an emotional St Andrew's when the announcement was made at half-time and he received a standing ovation. Unfortunately Gil died on 3 February 2010 at the age of 88 but at least he had been recognised by the club for being a great servant. (Note: Being Blues they spoilt the party by losing 1-2 in front of 24,825 supporters, Keith Fahey scoring the goal on 67 minutes.)

But to finish this story let's go back to our first meeting in March 1993 when I had to correct her about the fact that Blues had not gone into administration. So imagine my disappointment when reading Chapter 4 entitled 'Entering a Man's World' I find the following quotes:

Page 65: '.....*and then I saw the ad for Birmingham City, which was in administration and, as I'd discover, just right.*'

Page 71: '*Birmingham City was in administration when I took over and heading for oblivion.*'

Page 75: '*We couldn't say we were the best run club in the league because we were in administration.*'

So nearly 20 years after the event Baroness Brady of Knightsbridge is still getting it wrong and as a businesswoman should really know better.

Steve Claridge remembers:

> Karren [Brady] could also be really tight when it came to money, as my contract negotiations with her always revealed. That season we reached the final, against Carlisle United, of the Auto Windscreens Shield after seven tough games, during which I scored four goals. We were going down to Wembley for the Friday and Saturday nights before the game on Sunday, but Karren announced that the club would only pay for one night at our hotel, The Swallow at Waltham Abbey.
>
> Luckily Barry [Fry] found a wealthy friend who sponsored our second night, saving us £40 each. We were also only allowed to buy – buy not receive – ten tickets for our friends and relatives. The club said that because tickets were so scarce, with our amazing 55,000 allocation out of 76,000 revealing the depth of our support, players should pay. That added to the dissatisfaction that we were on a bonus of only £1,000, with all that extra revenue coming in. On top of that we each had to pay £8 for our club tie. Things like that knocked you back, undermined your morale. When you

are doing badly, you expect nothing, you just get your head down and get on with things. But when you are doing well you expect to be treated well with things like perks. And we did do well, winning the trophy with a goal by Paul Tait – a true Blue, having grown up supporting the club – in sudden death extra time (as he had also done in an earlier match against Swansea). But even that could not pass without controversy, this being Birmingham City. We only knew about it the next day when we read the papers but Paul had lifted the trophy wearing a T-shirt saying 'Shit on the Villa'. We did not take any notice but everybody overreacted and there were a lot of problems at the club for a few days.

On one side of the city he was the dog's bollocks, on the other he was like Salman Rushie. He had to keep his head down for a while, which was a bit difficult for Taity as he is a very social animal. Actually he was beginning to settle down a bit and stay in a few nights by then, although this may have had something to do with the fact that he was barred from quite a few places...

Tales from the Boot Camps

Michael Dunford recalls:

'When Mark Ward (Blues 1994–95 63 appearances 7 goals) left Everton to join Blues in 1994 he conveniently forgot to return his BMW club car. Myself and Everton director Keith Tamlin travelled south to St Andrew's in an attempt to retrieve the vehicle. Initially we spoke to, as a matter of courtesy, Karren Brady, explaining why we were there in the hope of getting the car returned without any legal action being required. She was totally sympathetic to our position but understandably stated that this was purely a domestic matter between Everton Football Club and the player. The matter was eventually resolved and not totally to our satisfaction.'

In the *Birmingham Post* on Thursday 20 October 2016 Karren wrote an article entitled 'Our fondness for Cadbury's is more than a love of chocolate'.

'Certainly, much of what I've learnt about business came from my time here. In 1992, at the tender age of 23 (all right, I was never that tender), I was appointed managing director of Birmingham City FC and managed, by hook and by crook, to take the club from the brink of bankruptcy to being a viable business. I had to be very single-minded because we had to get control of the business: we were technically in administration and had run out of money. I worked 16 hours, seven days a week, and maximised every business opportunity I could. At the end of my first year we made a profit for the first time in the club's modern-day history and by 1997 I was able to float the business and became the youngest managing director of a plc in the UK.'

Just for the record, at the end of financial year 1993/94 the club posted a loss before taxation of £1,131,157.

7

Commercial Matters

MY SON, Ben, worked in the commercial department of the Blues under the management of Perry Deakin. He joined in the summer of 2003 as the new lottery and promotions manager. He recalls:

'I was there to get the new lottery and away ticket schemes operational. I did not get a holiday that summer as there was a lot of work to do to ramp things up for the following season. The idea was to offer value for money with a range of initiatives such as discounted coach travel in better vehicles. It was a great team of seven of us, three selling football hospitality, two selling conference and events, a customer care manager, me and Perry's personal assistant. I still keep in touch with Alan George, who now runs a very successful hospitality and events company call Gala and Russell Ashman who left Blues to go to Villa Park!

'As a Bluenose I had taken a drop in salary to join the commercial department but soon found out that in 2003 they were using 70s technology with a 70s mentality which made things really frustrating when you had come from a modern-thinking organisation. Nothing demonstrated that more than the Christmas cards for the Junior Blues.

'It was my involvement in this activity which convinced me I was in for an uphill struggle due to the lack of information technology. The Junior Blues database was three box files of application forms! There was no printed copy let alone a basic spreadsheet. But the objective was for every member of the Junior Blues to receive a Christmas card every year – nothing wrong with that but how it was achieved was bizarre. Every year I was there we would employ a temporary person to handwrite 200 Christmas cards and envelopes. Prior to my joining this had been going on for three years and the box files had never been updated which meant that those members that had not renewed their membership got a card and those that had renewed got more than one card because their renewal application form had just been put in the box file.

'For the two years I was there Perry Deakin was a good motivational boss but never delivered on his promises of salary increases and it seemed to me that he had a problem with people leaving his department because no matter who it was or the reason for them leaving he always ended up bad mouthing their characters. This was a shame because the commercial team that was there during my time worked six days a week for a club they loved and each of us hoped to make a positive difference as there was a certain glamour in working for a Premier League club.

'The away travel club I set up had 3,000 members who paid £50 per year. This guaranteed an away ticket for any game plus 25 per cent discount on coach travel and a ten per cent discount at Roadchef cafes. Typical of Blues in those days, we were always looking to improve revenue and profitability and some of the enforced changes to the above membership benefits caused some irritation to genuine fans and understandably I took the abuse.

'The lack of an adequate database always caused problems; at the time we had 5,000 season ticket holders but it was never up to date. So if John Smith, who was on the database bought three tickets for his mates, the information on the three friends never got on the database so we never knew all our customers. The club always had the mentality, if there was a choice between £1 today and £10 next week it would always choose £1 so there was never going to be an investment in IT.

'My worst experience during my time at Blues was when it was alleged that I fell asleep at my desk. It was the day after the club's Christmas party which had been held at Mechu in Summer Row, Birmingham. The party involved both players and commercial staff and I must have had a number of champagne cocktails in the company of Matt Upson who seemed to have taken to Alan George and myself as he was buying!

'It was a late night/early morning and I don't remember much until I woke up on the sofa in Suzanne Johns's (conference and events manager) flat. Although I felt rough I got up and went into the office which was empty, it was like the *Marie Celeste*. Apart from Suzanne Johns, Nicola Beddowes and Perry's secretary Christina there was no one in, everyone had phoned in to say they were ill and that included Mr Deakin!

'It was alleged that I fell asleep at my desk, well I was only resting my eyes and I was at Suzanne's desk when there was this loud banging on the desk. It was Karren Brady. "I hope you're not asleep," she said, to which I replied, "I doubt it as I'm talking to you." At this point she stormed off and two minutes later I get a call from Perry. "Were you asleep at your desk?" he asked. "No, I wasn't and where are you?" I replied. That was not a well thought out response and Perry told me to get myself home as Karren was furious. There was nothing more said which belies the rumour all around the club that Karren had sacked someone for being asleep at their desk!

'Most members of the commercial team felt that Old Stand at St Andrew's (now the Ezegroup stand) was haunted.

Many of us experienced an uneasy feeling over there and on occasions heard footsteps even though the place was empty. Like all good ghost stories nothing can ever be proved one way or the other.

'One special and humorous event was when Russell and I had gone to Morrisons to get some lunch. We returned to the ground laden with cheese and onion batches, crisps and ham and when we approached the door, who was waiting to come out but Christophe Dugarry. Even though we had our hands full we managed to open the door for him. It's not every day you get to go to Morrisons and open the door for a World Cup winner!'

Perry Deakin was an interesting character and was the second person in a non-playing role in a football club to tell me within the first few minutes of our inaugural meeting that he 'played a bit'. The other had been Samesh Kumar.

The purpose of my initial meeting with Perry was to seek support for my book idea to celebrate the centenary celebrations of St Andrew's in 2006.

We met at St Andrew's in February 2005 when I outlined the concept and requested that the club might wish to be associated with the publication and if not, at least give me permission to use the logo.

Perry seemed genuinely interested and promised to get back to me after discussing it with his team. I was disappointed to receive a letter from him on 15 February stating, 'Unfortunately I cannot grant licence for you to use club logos, badge or marks in the presentation of the publication. This will conflict with club activities of a similar nature and although I wish you luck with your venture, no permission is granted.' He signed it 'commercial director' although he was not formally appointed to the board until 4 July 2005.

Although I cannot prove it I am pretty sure that Perry had no intention at the time of our meeting to produce a book to celebrate the centenary of St Andrew's, because his interest in my format was too intense if the club had already had plans in this direction. So it was no surprise to me that the club collaborated with Hyder Jawad, a local journalist at the time, together with his employers Trinity Mirror to bring out *Keep Right On – The Official Centenary of St Andrew's.*

In my opinion Perry was one of those people who thought it was a good idea if it was their idea. That was certainly the case regarding the Bluenose Executive Lunch Club. I invited him to attend our lunches where he would have got to meet a number of local businessmen who could have supported the club through sponsorship or other commercial activities. Not surprisingly Perry declined my invitation, even though it was a revenue-generating opportunity.

Later, as part of the evolution of the Bluenose Executive Lunch Club, I decided to run events to the fans based on a ticket price of £10 per head, as I felt that the club was only catering for corporate clients through its excellently organised dinners. There was nothing for the average fan who wanted to meet his heroes, have a few beers and still get change from a £20 note.

The editors of the *Blues* magazine were very supportive and whenever appropriate they carried an advertisement for my events. I was regularly attracting over 200 people to my events and it was obviously brought to the attention of Perry because their promotion included a flyer for the 'Return of The Penguins' event in their April 2005 edition, followed by a coloured quarter-page advertisement for 'Tom Ross and Friends' in the summer of 2005. A further quarter-page advertisement appeared in the September 2005 edition featuring 'The Re-birth of The Blues' and they also included my signing events in their feature 'The Month Ahead' in the December 2005 magazine.

In March 2006 the magazine promoted my ill-fated 'Evening with Frank Worthington' which was due to be held on 26 April but regrettably was cancelled due to poor ticket sales. As loyal as ever, Ian Drew and Eric Partridge ran an article on my first book, *The Blues – Great Games, Great Teams, Great Players* in their April 2006 issue but their continued support drew the wrath of Perry Deakin.

Thinking I was in competition with the club, which I was not, he put pressure on Ian and Eric to stop promoting the Bluenose Executive Lunch Club or he might restrict their access to the club and its players. Understandably they took him seriously and no more promotion was available to me.

Perry resigned from the board on 31 May 2007 and later joined Derby County in August 2007 as commercial manager. After a short time at Pride Park he disappeared from view and was a director of Indigo Sport Limited which was dissolved on 30 April 2008.

He later joined Port Vale as chief executive, before declaring himself bankrupt in August 2015. In February 2016 the supporters of Port Vale launched a lawsuit for a claim of misfeasance, a criminal act based on wilful inappropriate action or advice. The club went into administration in 2012 and after being appointed stadium manager at Oxford United in April 2012, just over a year later he was appointed as a consultant to Bury FC.

At one stage Perry's LinkedIn profile had a few gaps, notably Derby County and Port Vale in the employment section. It read:

Wolverhampton Wanderers – Commercial Manager 2000-02.

Birmingham City – Sales & Marketing Manager 2002-07.

Northamptonshire C.C.C. – Deputy C.E.O. and Sales & Marketing Director 2008-11.

Consultant – 2012-2014.

Although there was a lot of unsubstantiated rumour that he placed contracts on inflated terms to suppliers with family connections, there is little doubt that he did a good job for the Blues as these financials demonstrate:

Breakdown of Turnover

Year	Match Receipts	Broadcasting Revenue	Commercial Activities	Turnover
1993	£2,220,678	£268,083	£631,883	£3,120,644
1994	£2,584,693	£121,651	£1,056,788	£3,763,132
1995	£4,616,208	£196,381	£1,129,082	£6,941,671
1996	£4,624,252	£379,947	£2,332,872	£7,337,071
1997	£4,464,029	£329,770	£2,828,387	£7,622,186
1998	£4,984,953	£245,701	£3,106,205	£8,336,859
1999	£5,041,713	£269,289	£3,120,223	£8,431,225
2000	£5,664,070	£527,615	£3,212,280	£9,403,965
2001	£7,28,330	£1,906,146	£4,152,237	£13,286,713
2002	£6,850,512	£3,273,023	£5,060,501	£15,184,036
2003	£16,822,849	£13,218,978	£6,438,369	£36,480,196
2004	£21,476,371	£16,724,405	£7,136,042	£45,336,818
2005	£20,869,620	£13,965,482	£7,870,833	£42,705,935
2006	£17,913,106	£13,983,708	£8,220,072	£40,116,886
2007	£11,379.040	£6,700,602	£6,959,338	£25,038,980
2008	£20,921,215	£18,955,828	£9,958,622	£49,835,665
2009	£5,313,556	£15,807,394	£6,388,269	£27,509,219
2010	£7,403,736	£41,896,723	£7,122,207	£56,422,666
2011	£9,142,297	£44,458,783	£7,851,529	£61,452,609
2012	£9,276,165	£21,031,038	£8,778,667	£39,085,870
2013	£4,201,504	£14,776,785	£5,219,730	£24,198,019
2014	£3,591,096	£11,982,515	£4,512,137	£20,085,748
2015	£3,976,420	£12,408,289	£4,663,816	£21,049,000

8

Blues Magazine

I HAD the great pleasure and privilege to interview 16 ex-Birmingham City players for the now-defunct *Blues* magazine.

The first edition was published in February 2003 and featured Christophe Dugarry on the cover. Originally it was published by Programme Master Limited (part of Profile Media Group) and cost £2.95.

When the publication was put up for sale I tried to buy it, but as usual with Blues' commercial people the long-term view was secondary to the initial up-front payment. The previous publishers paid an initial fee of £10,000 plus the net profits of the operation. My proposal was rejected because it did not have an initial fee but a vastly improved profit share element which meant that over a period of time the club would have made significantly more than the Programme Master deal.

The second publishers were Ian Drew and Eric Partridge, who beat me to securing the rights. Both were Bluenoses and regular attendees at the games, so the magazine was in good hands.

I featured in the July 2004 issue answering the following questions:

Q: *What do you think of the Emile Heskey and Muzzy Izzet signings?*

A: It illustrates the growing status of the Blues within the Premier League that two such high profile players have agreed to join. Both of them played extremely well against us last season and if those performances can be achieved consistently then the squad has definitely been improved.

Q: *What about some of the other players we've been linked with?*

A: Gronkjaer would be an exciting addition to our attack options as pace on the right-hand side of the field is something we lack. Danny Mills and Robbie Savage in the same dressing room would be interesting? I've never rated Mills as an international standard full-back and it would appear that his Leeds contract is more important than his football career. Having said that, number two is definitely an area where we need to strengthen.

Q: *Mikael Forssell has signed for another year. How important do you think that is?*

A: Vital as without him it is difficult to see where the goals will come from even with the signing of Heskey. It will be interesting to see how successful Mikael is next season now that the Premier League defenders have had a season to work him out!

Q: *Are you happy with the strength of the squad now?*

A: No. I think the only position where we are adequately covered is goalkeeper, assuming Nico Vaesen re-signs. The back four needs a right-sided defender as I think Martin Taylor has been bought to take over from Kenny Cunningham after this season. Another midfielder is required and a forward.

Q: *Are there any areas of the squad that still need strengthening?*

A: With Purse, Hughes and Cisse leaving, Blues need to replace numbers otherwise we could be into the 'Horsfield as a defender scenario' again.

Q: *How do you think we'll do next year?*

A: Once again I think we will be at the mercy of injuries unless the squad is strengthened let alone improved. If Blues can maintain a top ten position and have no relegation fears after January then that will be tremendous because the Premier League is improving all the time.

Q: *Do you think we can make a serious challenge for Europe?*

A: No.

Q: *We went off the boil a bit at the end of last season. Does that worry you a bit?*

A: Yes it does for a number of reasons. It indicated the need for a bigger squad as it left Bruce with no options to change things around; at one stage the team literally picked itself, those that were fit played! Blues for all my 50 years have been underachievers and it has to stop; this season was the best chance of a cup final place, what happened? We blew it at home to a lower division side. This season we met Leicester at home after the worst week in their history and we didn't compete! We seemed to 'relax' once we were safe from relegation which puts a question mark around the ability of the management team to motivate the players!

Q: *Looking at the wider scene, how do you think we'll measure up to Villa next season?*

A: Villa will struggle next season and are my tip for relegation (as they have been for the last 50 years!). This season most of the talk will be about Doug Ellis and the ownership of the club. O'Leary will leave to fill O'Neill's seat at Celtic and we will get all six points!

Q: *And what about the Baggies?*

A: They will be relegated with Norwich and Crystal Palace!

In the January 2005 edition I was included in a feature entitled 'True Blue' when the fans had their say:

Name: Keith Dixon
Age: 58
Birthplace: Small Heath
Area you live now: Sheepy Magna, Warwickshire
Status: Married
Occupation: Director
Years as a Blues supporter: 50

Why did you start supporting Blues: My Dad took me once and that was it!

First Blues game seen 'live': A reserve fixture in 1953/54, John Schofield saved a penalty

Most memorable match: Blues v Liverpool League Cup Final 2001 what a day! What emotions!

Match you'd rather forget: 1956 FA Cup Final so much promised, so little delivered!

Best ever Blues goal: Stan Lazaridis v Everton last season

First favourite Blues player: Len Boyd (My dad used to cut his hair at his home)

Current favourite Blues player: Mario Melchiot

All-time favourite Blues player: Gil Merrick

Player you didn't want to see go (and why): Terry Hennessey – we should have built a team around him

Player you thought was a complete flop (and why): Ferdinand Coly – never seen someone so out of their depth on debut v Arsenal

Player you'd like to see in a Blues shirt next season: John Hartson – he frightens defenders and scorers goals regularly at all levels

Samesh and I signing the sponsorship contract

Samesh and I in the old boardroom overlooked by the Queen

Facing the press – Mike Wiseman, Jack Wiseman, myself and Bimal Kumar

Ian Clarkson leads out the team versus Notts County in the Triton kit for the first time

The advertisement which appeared in the *Financial Times*

Karren Brady wearing the second Triton kit

ROLDVALE LTD

Telephone: 0992 81 5151

Please reply to:
Birch Hall
Coppice Row
Theydon Bois
Essex CM16 7DR

Facsimile: 0992 81 5011

FACSIMILE TRANSMISSION

To: COLIN BURKE – LEORNARD CURTIS
From: KARREN BRADY
Date: 3RD MARCH 1993   **Pages:** 1
Subject: BIRMINGHAM CITY FOOTBALL CLUB

PRIVATE AND CONFIDENTIAL

Dear Colin,

Further to our telephone conversation, I can confirm my verbal offer of £600,000 for the 84% share of Birmingham City Football Club, the loan and any outstanding invoices from Kumar Bros Ltd to Birmingham City Football Club. We can sort out what is apportioned to what once the price has been agreed.

This offer of £600,000 made by Roldvale Ltd is subject to no material changes in the accounts up to the present date and contract.

We have put a great deal of thought into this offer, which is totally unnegotiable and expires at 12 noon on Friday 5 March 1993.

I look forward to hearing from you but direct telephone number is 071-253 2193.

Yours sincerely,

Karren Brady

KARREN BRADY

The fax from Roldvale making an offer for the Kumars' shares signed by Karren Brady

A dream come true – wearing a Blues shirt on St Andrew's

Legends on Tour – Ian Danter, Ian Clarkson, Robert Hopkins, Malcolm Page and Paul Tait

BELC at The Union with John Gayle and Joe Gallagher

Cheque presentation to Promise Dreams – Dave Dourass, myself, mascot and Steve Bull

Birmingham City All-Stars at The Lamb for my 60th - back row fourth from left Harry aged 13

Donation to Debra

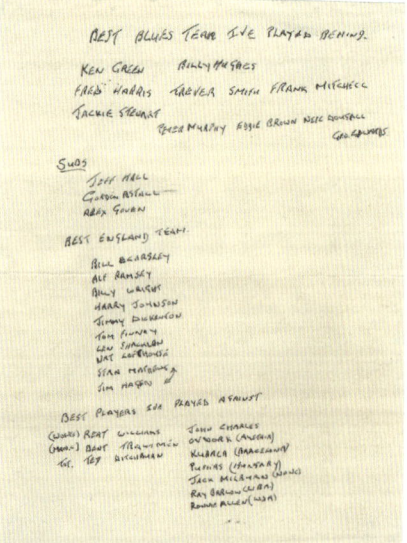

Gil names his best Blues and best England teams

Sheepy Old Boys at The Lamb for my 60th

My books on display in the BCFC Superstore – a proud moment

Gary Rowett faces the press with Colin Tattum seated on the far right

Trevor Francis leads out the teams assisted by his grandson

Signed Barry Fry poster

Academy scout identity card

Home dressing room

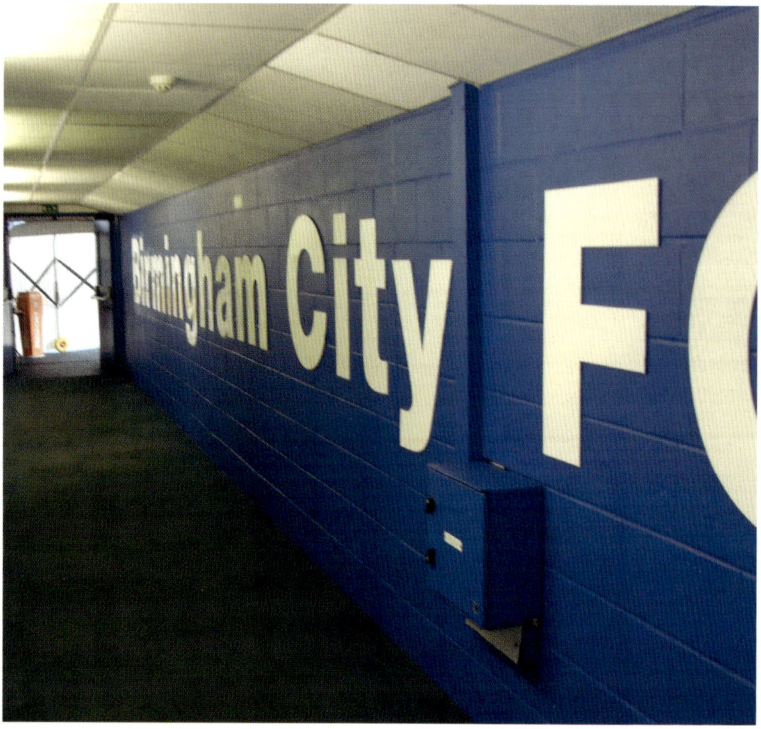
Birmingham City F

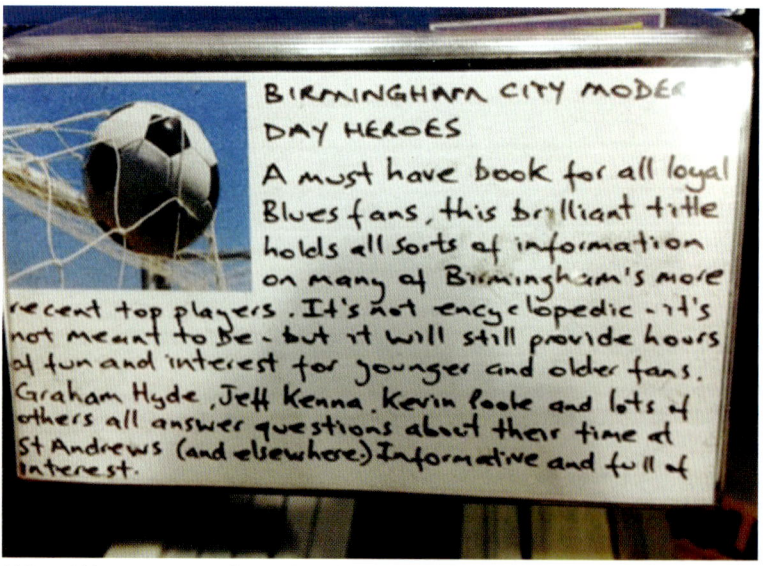

The first thing you see when you leave the home dressing room – the tunnel

BIRMINGHAM CITY MODE
DAY HEROES
A must have book for all loyal
Blues fans, this brilliant title
holds all sorts of information
on many of Birmingham's more
recent top players. It's not encyclopedic - it's
not meant to be - but it will still provide hours
of fun and interest for younger and older fans.
Graham Hyde, Jeff Kenna, Kevin Poole and lots of
others all answer questions about their time at
St Andrews (and elsewhere) Informative and full of
interest.

What Waterstones thought of Modern Day Heroes

Best ever individual performance: John Gayle in 1991 Leyland DAF Final

Six all-time favourite Blues players: Jimmy Bloomfield, Bertie Auld, Trevor Francis, Eddie Brown, Bob Latchford and Trevor Smith

Best ever Blues kit: The TRITON Showers 'raindrop' design (only joking but I was MD of Triton at the time and we got the blame for Samesh Kumar's design!)

Best thing about supporting the Blues: Having the same feeling of excitement and expectation going to a game at 58 that I had when I was eight

Worst thing about supporting the Blues: Nothing – it has to be better than supporting a suburb of Birmingham

Worst nightmare as a Blues fan: Being relegated on the last day of the season at Villa Park

Greatest ever Blues team: Merrick, Clarkson, Gallagher, Burns, Hawker, Page, Campbell, Tait, Pendrey, Hatton and Gayle: Subs: Francis K., Sprake (Why? all guests of the Bluenose Executive Lunch Club in 2004)

Best ever Blues manager: Gil Merrick – League Cup, European finals, who has achieved anything comparable?

In the November 2006 issue I contributed to its feature 'I WAS THERE', in which Blues fans shared their recollections of their most memorable matches. This was mine:

Birmingham v Tottenham Hotspur 6 January 1962
'I was just 15 on 6 January 1962 and the game was memorable as it was the first time my mate Ricky Dudley and I had been allowed to go to St Andrew's on our own. We had made the journey from Sheldon on the Corporation bus with limited funds and were full of youthful anticipation as we found a

spot leaning on a crash barrier on the Kop. This was pre-decimalisation when a ten bob note was a fortune and our budget was five shillings made up of two half-crowns, still that was enough to get in the game and get a "six of chips" on the way home!

'It was the third round of the FA Cup and the Blues were drawn against the mighty all-conquering Tottenham Hotspur, who had won the Double the previous season, becoming the first side to achieve that in the 20th century. 46,096 of us crowded into the terraces to glimpse the visitors from White Hart Lane: Blanchflower, Mackay, John White, Welsh wingers Medwin and Jones and of course, the goalscoring magician that was Jimmy Greaves.

'The Spurs came out with all guns blazing as they took a 3-0 lead within the first 30 minutes. St Andrew's was stunned but in those days "Keep Right On" meant exactly that and the noise was incredible. The players were made of stern stuff and the working-class heroes of Schofield, Lynn, Sissons,Hennessey, Smith, Beard, Hellawell, Orritt, Harris, Leek and Auld decided that enough was enough.

'Once Jimmy Harris had scored in the 33rd minute and again just after half-time, Ricky and I were swept along, literally, as the crowd went mad and a section got on to the pitch. I had never experienced the power of the crowd before and they compensated for the difference in class of the two teams. It was no surprise when Blues equalised through Ken Leek as Blues were the better team, taking the game to the champions.

'It was no surprise when we scored a "winning goal" and it was no surprise when it was ruled offside. The crowd went from hysteria to disappointment at the sound of the ref's whistle. The crowd was like a heart reacting to every nerve-shredding piece of action on the pitch but even it could not create the victory we deserved.

'For the record Spurs won the replay 4-2 and went on to retain the FA Cup by beating Burnley 3-1.

'The atmosphere that cold and bleak day was fantastic, the team had done us proud and together we had showed the true grit and determination of the Brummie. After the match a herd of young boys surrounded the Spurs team coach and I was lucky enough to stand on the wheel and pass my *Charles Buchan's Soccer Gift Book 1961/62* to the young Greaves who kindly found his picture on page 43 and signed it, getting the book back to me just before the coach began to move off.

'A great day was only marred by us missing the bus home and getting a real ticking off from our dads who were somewhat unimpressed with Jimmy's autograph, although 44 years later it is still in my possession!'

Then I was offered the opportunity to have my own feature in the magazine in which I would track down former players and interview them for 'My Time at Blues'.

My first subject was Ken Leek who I met at his home in Northamptonshire for the December 2006 edition.

The feature was a success with the readers and therefore I followed Ken's interview with:

Bobby Thomson in January 2007 – we met at The Plough in Harborne which was ill-advised as I didn't know then that Bobby is a reformed alcoholic.

February 2007 saw me in the home of Jimmy Harris, which is the house he was born in opposite Prenton Park, the home of Tranmere Rovers.

April 2007 saw me interviewing the then journalist Ian Clarkson in the café at the Solihull Library.

Colin Green featured in May 2007 via a telephone interview. Martin O'Connor was in the summer 2007 issue and we met at the pub at Muckley Corner.

For the August 2007 feature I travelled to Market Deeping near Peterborough to meet Bert Murray at his pub The Bull.

The following month it was Martin Thomas, followed in October with a trip to Formby to interview Howard Kendall in Alan Stubbs's wine bar Woodwards over the largest glass of white wine I have ever seen. I was on coffee.

In November I travelled to the home of Fred Pickering in Blackburn, for the December feature I stayed closer to home and met with Tony Want in the Malt Shovel pub at the Stonebridge island on the A45.

In the first month of 2008 I interviewed Paul Devlin over a coffee in the Gordon Blue café in Birmingham's Jewellery Quarter. This was followed by Graham Hyde at Wast Hills, Gil Merrick at his home in Shirley and Dave Latchford in Starbucks in Solihull.

Another telephone interview resulted in Brian Sharples featuring in the final issue which was May 2008. Ian Drew had been the sole publisher/editor since October 2006, printing the magazine alongside his newspaper business in Melksham, Wiltshire.

Although Brian Sharples was my last published 'My Time at Blues' article, I did interview Paul Tait once again in Starbucks Solihull and although I submitted the article for publication, the magazine ran out of time after five years at £2.95.

9

The Bluenose
Executive Lunch Club

THE IDEA of the Bluenose Executive Lunch Club, thereafter christened 'BELC' (pronounced belch), which was a convenient acronym for an eating and drinking organisation, came to me over the Christmas period of 2003.

It was to be a free membership club of businessmen (or those who could get a two-hour lunch break) who would meet monthly for lunch with a Birmingham City 'hero'. The only cost to the members would be their share of the food and drink bill, which would include that of the guest.

The initial members were Steve and Dave Dourass, Mark and Paul Luton, Steve Wragg, Brian Storer, Tom Gavin, Nic Hart, Eric Partridge, Ray Stilgoe, Martyn West, Richard Pocklington, Mark Jones, Jim Beeston, Steve Dann, Dave Hall, Graham Hill, Bob Benbow, Andrew Taylor, Mike and Trevor Thorley, Mark Belcher, Adam Bewley, Ian Drew, Darren Parker-Mead, Ashley Yeates and Neil Thorogood.

Our first guest was Ian Clarkson on 10 February 2004 at The Cross Café in Moseley. The Cross was owned by the Thorley brothers, who also provided at that time the catering at the Wast Hills training facility.

Our second event was held on 2 March 2004 at China Red on Broad Street in Birmingham, which was Gil Merrick's first experience of a Chinese meal!

For the next eight lunches we returned to The Cross Café and in the months from April to November 2004 we entertained in order: Bob Hatton, Kevin Francis, Malcolm Page, Garry Pendrey, Phil Hawker, Paul Tait, Alan Campbell and Gary Sprake.

On 8 December we moved to The Union in Mere Green (yes, I know that's Villa territory but I was acting as a non-executive director for Modern British Taverns Limited and as The Union was one of our businesses it made sense to take our business there), and we started with a double-header with John Gayle and Joe Gallagher.

The following year started on 11 January at Jefferson's in Solihull in the early evening. Why? So we could accommodate our guest, Robert Hopkins, who lived locally and was reluctant to travel to Villa territory. That was the only meeting we had where no food was required!

We returned to The Union on 1 February when our guest was Kenny Burns, who announced on his arrival that he had just got his driving licence back and got four numbers on the National Lottery. Kenny signed our guest book with the statement, 'Greatest Team of All and Supporters, Best wishes Kenny Burns'. Our heroes continued to accept my invitations and we celebrated 17 consecutive lunches at The Union featuring Ron Wylie, Noel Blake, John Schofield, John Vincent, Tony Evans, Brian Roberts, Mick Halsall, Kevan Broadhurst, Ian Atkins, Martin Thomas, Dave Latchford, Tony Want, Martin O'Connor, Des Bremner, Paul Devlin, Phil Summerill and Graham Sissons.

In October 2006 our venue moved the The Plough in Harborne where we lunched with Malcolm Beard, Bobby Thomson and Colin Gordon.

So BELC ended on 5 December 2006 simply because we 'ran out' of ex-Blues players living locally.

It was a great experience for me and every guest gave their time totally free of charge, not even asking for their travel expenses. Without doubt they are a superb bunch of guys!

In 2005 I decided to extend the club's involvement with ex-players and decided to organise evening events at the E57 Club in Birmingham to raise funds for Promise Dreams, a Midlands-based charity that helps to make dreams come true for terminally ill children.

The events we ran that year were:

27 April – 'The Return of the Penguins' featuring Kenny Burns, Joe Gallagher, Garry Pendrey, Johnny Vincent and Tony Want. The place went into uproar when, unknown to me and the audience, John Mitchell, the former Fulham striker turned up. He had knocked Blues out of the 1975 semi-final of the FA Cup with an agonising late goal. Mitchell untidily bundled the ball over the line despite the efforts of Joe Gallagher. That night was the first time they had met since that fateful event.

22 June – 'Tom Ross and Friends'

As a friend of Tom's, David Gold attended the above event together with the original FA Cup which he had bought to ensure it stayed in England. He refers to the occasion in his 2006 book entitled *Pure Gold – My Autobiography – The Ultimate Rags to Riches Tale*. In it, he recounts the following story about how Birmingham had finally landed the FA Cup:

'I also went to a working men's club in Birmingham where I do a question-and-answer session every couple of years with Tom Ross, the local radio presenter, as the host. As he finished with the players, two exes and one current, he called me on to the stage as the next guest. Out came the cup, rather like another guest, and everyone rushed forward to have a closer look. Such was the interest that afterwards

Tom announced the first ten out of the raffle could have their picture taken for £10.

'Then he had 20 people at £20 a head, and eventually we raised over £500, and this at a working men's club! And it didn't finish there. When Tom called a halt to the event, one man rushed forward and was so desperate to have his picture taken with the cup that he offered another £250!

'This, for me, showed the absolute passion roused by this inanimate object. I have, of course, been ribbed mercilessly by everyone in football, telling me Birmingham couldn't win it so we had to buy it. But I do believe we have the ability to win a trophy, and it would be unbelievable if it was the FA Cup.'

David Gold spent £478,000 on the oldest surviving FA Cup which was made for the 1896 final. Ultimately he donated it to the National Football Museum in Preston.

28 September – 'The Re-birth of the Blues' featuring Barry Fry along with Ian Clarkson, Robert Hopkins, Dean Peer and Ian Rodgerson.

On 26 and 27 November I ran BELC signing sessions in the sports section of the Memorabilia Show at the NEC. On both days I had Joe Gallagher, Malcolm Page and Gary Sprake signing photographs for the fans and they were augmented with Gil Merrick on the Saturday and John Gayle on the Sunday.

At each event we raised money through ticket sales, raffle, Heads 'N' Tails, Irish bingo and an auction. We also earned commission on the sales generated by allowing Danny Drewery of Midlands Memorabilia to have a shop within the venue. I always kept it quiet that Danny was a Villa fan.

In that year we raised over £2,000 for the charity, which was based in Wolverhampton and benefitted from the support of local celebrities such as Don Goodman, Steve Bull and Suzi Perry.

On 4 October 2006 I organised a further event at the E57 Club, a reunion of the 1963 League Cup-winning team. It was a great night featuring Gil Merrick, Colin Green, Brian Sharples, Mike Hellawell, Ken Leek and Bertie Auld. I also invited Bobby Thomson to attend as he was a member of the losing finalists – Aston Villa.

On 23 April 2008 I took 'The Blues Legends on Tour' to the Co-op Sports and Social Club in Yardley. The legends were Malcolm Page, Paul Tait, Ian Clarkson and Robert Hopkins and the event was hosted by Ian Danter.

10

Former Players' Association and Birmingham City All-Stars

THE FORMATION of the Birmingham City Former Players' Association is the culmination of a dream that Kevan Broadhurst and Tom Ross had for many years. It all started with the formation of the Blues All-Stars charity fundraising team of ex-players in 1991.

That first team included Kevan, Joe Gallagher, Micky Evans, Tom Ross, Terry Cooper, Ron Green, Trevor Morgan, Garry Pendrey, Robert Hopkins, Tony Evans, Tony Taylor and Steve Lynex to name but a few. Over the years, the Blues All-Stars have raised over £1m for many deserving charities around the Birmingham area.

Eventually Kevan and Tom discussed the logistics of establishing a formal Former Players' Association. The football club bought into the idea and with the great help of committee member Jessica Birch and the club's head of corporate sales, Adrian Wright, the association, which now boasts over 200 members, was formed. The aim was to find as many ex-players as possible. The major reason for the association is to build a bridge between the club, the supporters and its history. It also allows the ex-players to keep in contact with each other. By virtue of pitch and hospitality appearances, the ex-players can also keep in touch with the fans.

The association believes that every single player who has worn the royal blue shirt should be recognised and made welcome at St Andrew's.

Launch date was Friday 25 April 2008 with a special gathering at St Andrew's which included Alan Ainscow, Alex Govan, Colin Green, Bob Hatton, Bobby Thomson, Dave Latchford, Dennis Isherwood, Eddie Brown, Geoff Cox, George Allen, Gil Merrick, Gordon Astall, Graham Hyde, Ian Atkins, Jon Bass, Kevin Poole, Mick Halsall, Noel Blake, Paul Peschisolido, Ron Wylie, Tony Rees, Jon McCarthy, Malcolm Page, Nicky Eaden, Pat Wright, Peter Warmington, Steve Robinson, Keith Bertschin, Martin O'Connor, Ian Clarkson, Paul Brady, Phil Hawker, Tommy Mooney, Joe Gallagher, Kevin Ashley, Mick Darrell, Nigel Gleghorn, Paul Hendrie, Robin Stubbs and Tony Coton.

On 21 May 2009 I met with Tom and Kevan at The Belfry Hotel in Sutton Coldfield to discuss my ideas to generate funds for the FPA through a number of events and activities to be organised and implemented by myself on a 50/50 profit share basis. As the FPA had been formally constituted and the Bluenose Executive Lunch Club had ceased operations in 2006 I felt that the time was right for me to be appointed as a BCFC FPA official fundraiser.

It was clear that Birmingham City would continue to host formal dinners at St Andrew's using FPA members, but there was a demand for 'unofficial' events, whereby the fans could meet their heroes in an informal environment at an affordable cost with a target of £10 a head.

The idea was that former players would be paid for their time and travel expenses when attending an event but also that it would be an enjoyable experience for them including something to eat and drink. While these costs reduced the resultant profit pot for the FPA it did ensure that the ex-players were properly reimbursed for their time and everything was organised in a business-like manner.

At the time it was not the intention for me to become a member of the FPA committee, although I was formally appointed in 2012. Up until then I attended meetings to present progress reports, which included an 'open accounting' process to enable the committee to fully understand the cost basis of each event and the potential contribution to the finances. At the end of each three-month period I produced a financial statement and a cheque for 50 per cent of the profit generated.

The events held were:

16 September 2009 – 'The Promotion Years' at E57 Club, Birmingham. Hosted by Tom Ross who interviewed Malcolm Page, Robert Hopkins, Paul Tait, Ian Clarkson and Lee Carsley.

14 October 2009 – 'Autowindscreen' at E57 Club, Birmingham. Hosted by Ian Danter who interviewed Mark Ward, Dave Barnett, Paul Tait and Peter Shearer.

18 November 2009 – 'An Evening With Bertie Auld' at Redditch United Football Club. Hosted by Tom Ross.

18 March 2010 – 'An Evening with Barry Fry' at Redditch United Football Club. Hosted by myself because Tom Ross sent his apologies having being diagnosed with diabetes.

27 May 2013 – 'League Cup – 50th Anniversary' at St Andrew's Legends Lounge. Hosted by Tom Ross, featuring Bertie Auld, Mike Hellawell, Winston Foster, Jimmy Harris, Colin Green and Brian Sharples. This was the last event for

which I took total responsibility. It was such a success that before the event started, stadium manager Ian Pugh came up to me concerned that I had breached the maximum number of guests limit set by the fire insurance company. For a short period the event was in danger of being called off but after a count on the tickets sold and agreeing the number of guests and committee members he allowed the event to start.

The 1963 heroes were booked into the Inkford Hotel on the Alcester Road in Wythall, where most of them had stayed for a previous event. For the seven rooms plus the bar bill it cost £395. This is one of the things you get from the ex-players – they do not expect the world in terms of payment or comfort and are just happy to re-connect with the club and the fans. Liam Daish stayed at the Royal George in Garrison Lane for the princely sum of £40, for a luxury double room. Thanks go to the McGroarty family who own the Royal George for all their support over the years.

One of the disappointments surrounding these type of events is the way so-called supporters try to sidetrack them by standing outside the venue to get several autographs from each individual player which are clearly destined for eBay or the like. Typically the players do not like to say no so they stand outside signing away, which means their time in the bar is reduced or worse still the start is delayed. When the cost of entry is only a tenner I think this behaviour is unreasonable so I began meeting the players on their arrival to get them straight into the event. I asked a number of former players the question, 'What does the Former Players' association mean to you?'

Gil Merrick:

'For years since my retirement from football and Birmingham City, I have thought the ex- players needed an association this is the best thing that has happened for the former players.'

Alex Govan:

'The Former Players' Association means the world to me, it's nice to meet up with old friends who I haven't seen for years. Birmingham City has always looked after me well.'

Bob Hatton:

'It's great to come back to St Andrew's and see my old team mates and stars from previous generations who I looked up to and respected. The FPA is a great idea and should have been started years ago! Long may it continue and let's hope it goes from strength to strength.'

Ian Clarkson:

'The Former Players' Association is a great way of socialising with former mates, having a game of football and raising money for good causes.'

Trevor Francis:

'I would like to pay tribute to Tom Ross and Kevan Broadhurst on helping to put this together, something very much overdue and it's a great idea and opportunity for all players from all generations to get together to see each other to share memories and stories from BCFC. I applaud them both on their achievement.'

Gordon Astall:

'I don't get many opportunities to catch up with my playing mates. It's great there is now an association which brings together players from all different generations who can share stories and enjoy memories of Birmingham City Football Club.'

In August 2015 the existing committee of Tom Ross, Kevan Broadhurst, Dean Holtham, Mike Wiseman and myself were augmented with the appointment of Malcolm Page and Jeff Kenna, which meant that the committee had three former players of BCFC to further represent their colleagues' interests. Pete Hall joined at the same time to assist on the commercial side of our activities.

Malcolm Page wrote to the members of the FPA and said, 'At the start of 2016 Kevan Broadhurst put to your committee the notion that it would be a fantastic idea to say a big thank you to all, or as many as possible of our former players.

'A thank you for those who take time out to play and raise money for charities on a Sunday, give time to personal appearances either at matches or any committee organised events, also for just being part of a fantastic group of former colleagues. So it was at that time the foundations were put in place and further developed at our meetings as the year went on. Thank you to all our committee for making this event possible.

'So it all finally came together on September 30 2016 with golf at the Olton Golf Club, Solihull. A celebration and prize-giving dinner at the St John's Hotel and overnight accommodation for those who wished to. Then the following day with an invitation from Birmingham City FC to have lunch and watch the match against Blackburn Rovers at St Andrew's. Quite a feast!!

'A big thank you to Olton Golf Club for giving us such a warm welcome from friendly staff and for presenting the golf course in such an immaculate condition.

'Would the weather be good? It plays such an important part in these events and thankfully on this occasion it was brilliant!

'Limit on buggies could have been a worry. However the few who have felt the rigours of a number of years on a football pitch again pulled together as always and shared as best they could. Importantly no complaints from Mick Harford!!

'The golf was exceedingly competitive as you would expect and as the weather was good it reflected the excellent scores all round, however one score by a member of the former players stood out above all others!!

'For those of you who don't understand the Stableford points system (I'm not surprised if you don't) in simple terms you get so many points for completing the hole in so many shots!

'To go around in par would equate to roughly 36 points! What did this Rory McIlroy do? Only 45 points!!!

'Anyway, many congratulations to Dean Holtham for winning the best individual score prize. I fancy a sneaky visit to Olton Golf Club a week before might have helped!!

'We had players representing the **60s**: Geoff Vowden, Bert Murray, Bobby Thomson, Malcolm Page; **70s**: Les Phillips, Kenny Burns, Jimmy Calderwood, Paul Hendrie, Peter Withe; **80s**: Alan Ainscow, Keith Bertschin, Kevin Dillon, Phil Hawker, Tony Coton, Mick Harford, Guy Russell, Carlo Rossi, Phil Sproson; **90s**: Paul Devlin, Richard Scott, Liam Daish, Andy Harris; **2000s**: Dele Adebola, Jeff Kenna, Peter Gilbert and even creeping into the **2010s** Maik Taylor. If we include our spectators Jackie Lane and Les Dolphin it takes in the **40s** and **50s**!!! Amazing!

'Thank you to all the former players who were able to join us on the golf course that day and we were so pleased you enjoyed it so much!

'The challenge in the years to come is to keep this thing going and the only way forward is to invite new and younger players to the group!

'The golf over it was time for a bit of banter in the bar afterwards before heading the five minutes down the road to the bar at St John's Hotel (it's a hard life).

'We were hardly halfway through our day, with the evening and Blues match still to look forward to!

'As well as our hard-working committee this day could not have happened without the major part our sponsors played so thank you so much to Office Furniture, Clarity Copiers, Traffix, Voozo Dealer Hollywood Monster, the PFA and Mike Turl of Solihull Moors for supporting the day and help giving former players an enjoyable and memorable occasion in which to meet up and share stories of "then" and "since" together.'

In 2012 I secured my first external sponsor in the form of Nailcote Hall Hotel in Balsall Common. The deal was for £500 and was to include shirt sponsorship of the All-Stars, but regrettably we did not get our act together and Rick Cressman was magnanimous enough to refuse our offer of a £200 refund.

On 9 March 2012 there was a second induction into the Legends Hall of Fame including Roger Hynd, Ian Bennett, Alex Govan, Malcolm Page, Robert Hopkins, Garry Pendrey and much to his surprise, as he knew nothing of it until the night, Kevan Broadhurst.

In the winter of 2013 we successfully held a 'Back to the 80s' night with Frank Worthington, Howard Gayle, Tony Coton, Noel Blake, Kevin Dillon, Brian Roberts, Garry Pendrey, Robert Hopkins, Keith Bertschin, Joe Gallagher, Malcolm Page, Kevin Ashley, Des Bremner, Kevan Broadhurst, Guy Russell, Ian Clarkson and Phil Hawker. The beneficiary of the night was Alan Ainscow who had been ill for some time.

Themed evenings are our style so we had two 1990s events, the first headlined by Barry Fry on 21 March 2014 and the second with Trevor Francis, who we knew would be late as his plane from Dubai did not land until 6pm in Heathrow. He turned up very tired and was brilliant! That was 24 October 2014. The event was reported on in the

BCFC matchday programme, in the feature 'Royal Blue Forever':

'The Former Players' Association and BCFC put on another successful reunion night, sponsored by our great friends, Pure Cloud Solutions, at the end of the month. This time it was 'Back to the 90s Part Two' with Trevor Francis as the main speaker. It was another spectacular evening with Dele Adebola, Bryan Hughes, Paul Peschisolido, Martin O'Connor, Michael Johnson, Martin Thomas, Darren Carter, Richard Forsyth, Garry Pendrey and Kevan Broadhurst all in attendance.

'On the night we raised a sizeable sum of money for the British Polio Fellowship in memory of the legendary Jeff Hall, who died from polio in 1959. After a brilliant meal, TF was interviewed on stage by the MC, Tom Ross, the FPA chairman and Free Radio's head of sport. Trevor was superb and kept the audience engrossed, as befits a genuine living legend. He spoke passionately about his lifetime love affair with the club and the fans and offered to do anything he possibly could to help BCFC in the future. He also talked about his pride in being awarded a star on the Broad Street Walk of Fame and how honoured he was that it would be presented on "Trevor Francis Day" at St Andrew's for the home game with Nottingham Forest on 29 November.

'Then it was the turn of the players to answer questions with O'Connor, Johnson, Peschisolido and Carter all providing an entertaining insight into the life of a Blues player. Professional auctioneer Graham Birch conducted the auction to raise much-needed funds for the FPA and Polio Fellowship. Club officials Panos Pavlakis, Julia Shelton and Ian Dutton were part of the audience, while FPA committee members Dean Holtham, Keith Dixon and Mike Wiseman were also in attendance. In summary it was an amazing fun-filled night with some great guys and fantastic supporters.'1

Prior to my involvement with the Former Players' Association I had already benefitted from its generosity in turning out for me in favour of several charities with which I was associated.

The first occasion was on 16 August 1998 when the Blues All-Stars turned out against my team at the time, the Sheepy Old Boys at the ground of Atherstone United.

Sheepy Old Boys is still going today under the original management of Clive Blewitt and I was a fringe player, making my final appearance just before my 60th birthday, but more of that later.

We kicked off at 11am and made the mistake of taking the lead through a screamer from Richard Pocklington midway through the first half. Up until that point the All-Stars had been 'playing nicely' but at that point they went up a few gears and eventually won 7-1.

The programme stated the All-Stars squad as anyone from this list: Dave Latchford, Kevan Broadhurst, Robert Hopkins, Ian Atkins, Kevin Ashley, Keith Downing, Joe Gallagher, Geoff Scott, Paul Harding, Mickey Clarke, Paul Brady, Richard O'Kelly, Arthur Mann, Brian Roberts, Tony Evans, Phil Hawker, Paul Hendrie, Steve Lynex, Keith Bertschin and Tom Ross.

The Sheepy Old Boys had just one ringer and that was the owner of Atherstone United, Ku Akeredolu.

Further events were staged:

Sunday 15 April 2007 at The Lamb, Tamworth. Kick-off 11am

We raised nearly £1,500 for our nominated charity Debra for 2007. The teams were:

Sheepy Old Boys: John Shelton-Smith, Mark Evans (Mark Evans Estate Agents – sponsor), Richard Williams, John Holcroft (San Giovanni – sponsor of All-Stars), Trevor Bourne, Clive Blewitt, Ian Goodship, Phil Luke, Gary Mills (Tamworth manager), Darron Gee (Tamworth assistant manager), Neil Sheasby, Justin Jagger, Rob Timmins, Baz Suffolk and Brian Greenfield.

All-Stars: Tom Ross (manager), Ian Clarkson, Andy Harris, Harry Dixon (13 years old), Keith Dixon (60 years old), Alan Kurilla, Tony Workman, Dave Busst, Phil Hawker, Kevan Broadhurst, Robert Hopkins, Martin O'Connor, Mickey Clarke, Paul Devlin, Graham Hyde and Dean Holtham.

Sunday 21 October 2007 at Atherstone United, kick-off 11.30am v Emmerdale

The Emmerdale squad included Ben Freeman (Scott Windsor), Jim Hooton (Sam Dingle), Kelvin Fletcher (Andy Sugden), Cleveland Campbell (Danny Daggert), Glen Lamont (Ritchie Carter), and Steven Farebrother (John McNally).

Sunday 16 May 2010 v Witherley Veterans – managed by Ian Bates for 50th anniversary charity match. Raised £216 to be divided between Witherley village charities and the Air Ambulance

The great thing about the Blues' All-Stars which is never promoted is the fact that they do not charge the charity for their attendance, unlike the Aston Villa and West Bromwich Albion equivalents. All the Blues require is a decent pitch and facilities, and some post-match food and drink. Robert Hopkins always substitutes himself at half-time so he can have first go at the refreshments!

11

An Author

I KNOW it is said that everyone has a book within them but my reason for starting to write books on the Blues was motivated by our neighbours Aston Villa.

It used to annoy me that when I visited the sports section of any national book seller there were always more books on the Villa than Birmingham. I decided to change that and if you visit WH Smith and Waterstone's you will see that I have achieved my objective.

Periodically I visit stores to check on their stock of my books and in August 2016 at Waterstone's in Birmingham were six copies of *Modern Day Heroes*, three of *50 Greatest Matches*, one of *Bad Blood*, and seven of *Robbo – Unsung Hero*. Across the way in WH Smith were six copies of *The Leaders*.

Unless you are J.K. Rowling, books do not sell themselves and authors have to do their own marketing in retail outlets. It is a good idea to introduce yourself to the sports section manager/specialist and offer to sign any stocked items. Most consumers like to buy signed copies as opposed to blank copies and therefore retailers will put 'signed by author' stickers on their stock and openly promote the title. I enjoyed this unsolicited promotion from Waterstone's in Birmingham when I signed their stock of *Modern Day Heroes*.

This hand-written note was on the football shelf alongside my books, 'A must have book for all loyal Blues fans, this brilliant title holds all sorts of information on many of Birmingham's more recent top players. It's not encyclopaedic – it's not meant to be – but it will still provide hours of fun and interest for younger and older fans. Graham Hyde, Jeff Kenna, Kevin Poole and lots of others all answer questions about their time at St Andrew's (and elsewhere). Informative and full of interest.'

You are also required to attend book signing sessions but more of that later.

When you decide to write a book, the primary requirement is a recognised publisher for your subject. Fortunately for football books there are a number of specialist publishers but it is incredibly hard to break into this world of known authors who have long-term publisher relationships and a seemingly endless list of potential new book ideas. Publishers can only get so many books on to the market and if their requirements are being met by their existing stable of writers then why should they entertain a new entrant? The answer is they don't.

Among my rejection letters came a crumb of comfort that all was not lost. One publisher admitted that often they reject submissions because there is no evidence from the aspiring author that they can deliver!

Therefore I decided to go it alone and prove to any future publisher that I had a track record, albeit small, of being able to deliver a finished product.

I needed a reason to write a book and the centenary of St Andrew's was perfect timing in 2005. Elsewhere in this publication you will have read the outcome of my efforts to get the Blues' commercial department interested in supporting my efforts and as a result I knew I was on my own.

I found a printer/designer in Redditch that would charge me £1,000 for 100 books. In these pre-internet days it wasn't that easy to uncover alternatives so I went with them and published my very first book, *The Blues – Great Games, Great Teams, Great Players* as a Bluenose Executive Lunch Club publication in January 2006 to celebrate the centenary of St Andrew's.

Because of the rejection of support from BCFC I made a point of positioning the book as '100 per cent unofficial and totally unauthorised'. Gil Merrick provided the foreword and it featured 50 games, from the first in November 1875 up to the first in the Premier League on 18 August 2002. It included 61 illustrations and I sold copies from the boot of my car to friends, relatives and colleagues for £13.99. I was on my way and I had turned a profit.

Since then I have turned advisor to other aspiring authors and two books have been self-published by two friends of mine. *Dear Clementina – Letters From One Border Terrier Pup to Another* was signed by the author, Colin Burke, 'Thanks for the advice and encouragement', and at the opposite end of the spectrum is *The Anatomy of a Coal Mine – Daw Mill Colliery 1957–2013* which sounds like a specialist subject on *Mastermind* but my neighbour Bob Blenkinsopp asked me to look at his work and after minimal input from me he self-published successfully, signing my copy, 'To my very good friend and mentor!'

I was on my way but still without a publisher. I had met Bobby Thomson on a number of occasions at Bluenose Executive Lunch Club meetings and I had completed an article on him for *Blues* magazine. Bobby is a very enthusiastic man with lots of stories from a long and eventful career and life and I felt him worthy of a biography. We agreed to collaborate under Bobby's title *O by Whom* and I had to pitch the idea to a targeted publisher. I chose Breedon Books as they were local and specialised in local history and sport and had a track record of successful publications.

A pitch to a publisher, or submission, is not just a telephone call outlining your idea. It is quite a detailed process including the following and more:

- Proposed title and sub-title
- Description of the book in no more than 300 words
- A brief overview of the book and, if applicable, a list of chapters/sections
- Whether the book is already written, or an accurate timescale required to deliver the completed manuscript
- If the manuscript is completed, whether it's been edited, to what level and by whom
- Type of images; how many to be included
- Details of any previously published written work

Bobby and I met in a number of locations including The Plough, Harborne, Priory Tennis Club, and at his home where he amazed me with his football tales and his drinking adventures with the likes of George Best and Jimi Hendrix. Bobby was a reformed alcoholic and was great company while sipping his mandatory orange juice.

The project was coming along well and I had sent my submission to Steve Caron at Breedon so we were waiting upon a decision. I explained to Bobby that publishers review submissions at set times of the year and therefore we should not expect an immediate response. Bobby grew increasingly impatient and threatened to take his book to a friend of his, who claimed she could get it published straightaway. I asked Bobby to stay with me as Steve had promised me a decision as soon as possible.

Bobby refused so on 17 December 2007 I wrote to him and said, 'Please find enclosed a copy of all the correspondence to Breedon Books regarding the publication of your autobiography *O by Whom*. As requested the final contact is to conclude matters with Breedon Books i.e. to inform them that we do not want them to publish the book. As you know Breedon Books were my choice of publisher based on their track record in the field of football biographies and I share your disappointment that they have been so reluctant to make a decision on *O by Whom*.

'I would like you to take the existing manuscript to Shirley Thompson and any of your other contacts in the publishing world to see if you can get it published before 2009. Unfortunately I feel I cannot devote any further time to the project and wish you well with a new collaborator. Needless to say I will co-operate with anyone to bring this project to the bookshelf. A computer disk is enclosed on which is the manuscript and synopsis. I will return your scrapbooks etc early in the New Year.'

When I returned his property I mentioned that I hoped that if the book was published I would at least get an acknowledgement and Bobby agreed. It was published under the title *The Real Bobby Dazzler* by Simon Goodyear, who specialises in ex-Aston Villa players' biographies, without the promised acknowledgement. Ironically the book was published by DB Publishing, which was a reincarnation of the failed Breedon Books.

As we all know fate plays its part in our stories and when I rang Steve Caron to inform him of Bobby's decision he said before I had a chance to tell him the purpose of the call that he wanted to go ahead with Bobby's autobiography and had allocated me a publication deadline.

Imagine my disappointment, if only Bobby had hung on for a little longer. I decided not to inform Steve about Bobby's decision until I had given some thought to a better alternative subject for a football biography.

It did not take long for me to come up with the idea of Gil Merrick but I had to get his agreement before approaching any publisher. Having met Gil before, it was easy for me to set up a meeting at his home in Shirley, Solihull.

Persuading Gil was not easy on two counts; firstly he had already published a biography entitled *I See It All* in 1954 and therefore felt there was no appetite for another book about him, and secondly he had fallen out with BCFC over his sacking in the early 1960s which had resulted in him making the decision never to be involved in the club from that day forward.

I felt I could not overcome the second point but a lot had happened in his football career since 1954 including the FA Cup Final in 1956, European football, management, and Blues' only major trophy. He had a story to tell and thankfully he agreed.

At this stage I rang Steve Caron and explained Bobby's decision but that I had a strong alternative. To say he was delighted that Gil Merrick was replacing Bobby in his roster would be an understatement, and for the only time in my book-writing experiences I was paid an advance of £500 by a cheque dated 14 April 2009. The book was published in 2009 by Breedon Books a year before Bobby's own biography was out.

Gil was my all-time hero and therefore writing his biography was a dream come true. To be sitting in his lounge talking about his career was an absolute delight. He was a modest man and the only testimony at his home to his footballing life was a colour photograph of him playing for England which hung proudly in his hall. Nothing else, just one solitary item.

The book is arguably my most successful and is still selling some seven years later. I know this because twice a year I receive a royalty statement from my publisher. Amazon is a major influencer on book sales these days and publishes on-line top-selling lists by genre. In football books bestsellers,

Gil got to number 15 in the top 50, wedged between the Paul Scholes biography in 14th and *Brian Clough – 150 B.C.: Cloughie –The Inside Stories* in 16th. Gil was proud to be in such company.

Along with Ivan Barnsley's efforts for a reconciliation, I believe the raised profile gained for Gil following the publication of his biography led to the new owners wishing to engage with their most famous of players, which culminated in the renaming of the railway end of St Andrew's as The Gil Merrick Stand. Gil became a friend and provided me with two treasured mementos of our time together; a hand-written birthday card to celebrate my 60th birthday and a hand-written note regarding the best Blues and England teams with which he played.

My second book in 2009 was entitled *Birmingham City – 50 Greatest Matches* and again was published by Breedon Books. It was the last under that name, as due to financial difficulties Steve Caron put the business into administration and re-emerged under the name of Derby Books. The title of this book brought about a number of comments around the theme of, 'What's your next book? *250 great throw-ins?*'

When I was researching the Gil Merrick book I telephoned Jackie Sewell, who Gil had asked me to contact on his behalf for a comment or two. Jack (only the 'outside world' called him Jackie) was brief in his response, suggesting 'That's typical of Gil, he always was lucky, why doesn't someone write me story?' Clearly Jack had a story to write so I pitched the idea to Steve Caron and he was in favour.

So in 2010 Jackie Sewell's biography was published. It was an interesting project because unlike Gil, Jackie had memorabilia of his career all over the house. On my first visit to his modest home in Nottingham he took me into the spare bedroom which was full of boxes containing seemingly everything associated with his career; the complete Aston

Villa kit from the 1957 FA Cup Final, every shirt he had worn in internationals and a number of scrapbooks which his mother had started to compile at the beginning of his career.

This made my job so much easier and Jack gave me full access to all of it. But if only it had been Blues memorabilia instead of the Villa! I alerted Jack's son to the potential value of what was in his dad's back bedroom and that he should get it insured as the release of my book would alert people to what he had in his possession.

The arrangement between myself and my biography subjects is that we split the royalties generated and that is usually confirmed with a handshake. That wasn't good enough for Jack and I had to confirm it in writing. After two decent royalty payments I was notified by my publisher that they had had Jack on the telephone demanding that he was paid his share of the royalties direct. I was disappointed that he didn't trust me but didn't object as I felt he was not in a good position financially. That feeling was confirmed when in February 2011 it was reported that he had sold his Villa cup final shirt for £2,500.

Jack died on 26 September 2016 and I have two memories of our time together. Jack was convinced that England's 6-3 defeat by the Hungarians at Wembley in 1953 was due to one fact only; the FA selection committee's pre-occupation with picking players from the FA Cup-winning side, which in 1953 was Blackpool. Whether he was right or not is debatable but if you look at the England team that played before the Hungarian game and compare it with the side on that fateful day, you will see several changes involving Harry Johnston, Ernie Taylor, Stan Matthews and Stan Mortensen coming into the line-up. Who did they play for? Blackpool.

Jack loved Africa and he spent a large part of his time managing and coaching there, which at that time was unheard of in soccer terms. He was instrumental in establishing football in Africa which has resulted in so many African players performing in the Premier League these days.

Once again Steve Caron's business went into administration but once again he re-emerged under the banner of DB Publishing which continued to support my works: *Birmingham City Modern Day Heroes* in 2011; *Bad Blood* in 2013; *Robbo – Unsung Hero* and *The Leaders – Birmingham City* in 2015.

When *Bad Blood* was due for publication I took it to commercial director Ian Dutton to see if the club would promote and stock it. Without reading the book and therefore based only on the title, the club refused to offer any support, stating, 'It would damage the club's efforts to have a harmonious relationship with its near neighbours.' How out of touch could a club be from its fan base? There is not a single Bluenose that wants a 'harmonious relationship' with the Villa.

It is strange how things happen but shortly after the rejection I attended an ex-players' event in the Legends Lounge at St Andrew's. I was sitting with a number of my 'banned' books wrapped in brown paper (pre-orders from friends) when Tom Ross welcomed on to the stage Frank Worthington. As he approached the stage he orchestrated a loud rendition of 'Sh*t on the Villa' – so much for a harmonious relationship!

Not all my ideas have ended on the bookshelf. At the beginning of 2011 I was considering the subject of my next book and eventually thought a biography of Stephen Carr would be a good idea, not only for Blues fans but due to his time at Newcastle United and Tottenham Hotspur.

The problem was how to get the idea over directly to Stephen. Via Andy Walker, who at the time was PR and social media manager at the Blues, I got the telephone number of Carr's agent Rob Segal.

I spoke with Rob on 4 March. He agreed it was a good idea and they had already been approached by Harper Collins in a similar vein. However, he was worried about Stephen's ability to contribute, describing him as 'a good talker but doesn't like to talk'. Our conversation ended with me agreeing to e-mail him a business proposal.

After speaking with Steve Caron, my publisher, he suggested that one of the problems we would have could be the level of advance Stephen would expect based on his knowledge of the advance that was paid to Darren Anderton for his biography. It was agreed that my best option was to get Rob to do a deal with Harper Collins and for me to act purely as ghost writer.

Our proposal was forwarded to Stephen via Rob and it wasn't long before he replied that Stephen wasn't interested.

My publishers suggested that a new market was the e-book and they felt it was an opportunity to produce a piece that wasn't 60,000 words but a concise record of either a period in Blues' history or a personality associated with the club. I decided Jim Smith was a worthy candidate for my first e-book, under the working title of *Bald Eagle*. The project never got off the ground although I did have the pleasure of meeting Jim in the bar of The Bear Hotel in Woodstock, Oxfordshire, in March 2012 to discuss his time at the Blues. In the end, what was planned to be an hour prior to Jim flying out to Spain turned into two and a half hours of absolute delight.

I had known Tom Ross for some time through the Former Players' Association and my charity events with BELC but on one particular day he was different to me. It turned out he wanted to ask me a favour.

I was at St Andrew's for the Trevor Francis Day on Saturday 29 September 2014 with an 'access all areas' pass as I was spending a matchday with Paul Robinson for inclusion in our biography *Robbo – Unsung Hero* and unusually Tom wanted a conversation with me about my writing.

He was complimentary about the way I wrote because when he had read my biography on Gil Merrick he felt it was like listening to the great man himself. Quite a compliment. Anyway, he explained that he thought the time was right for him to write his story and he asked whether I would be prepared to help. I said that I would think about it and let him know early in 2015.

After some thought I decided to at least discuss the matter with Tom and our initial meeting took place at the offices of Free Radio in Brindley Place on 22 January 2015.

I used a mind-mapping technique to try and identify whether Tom had a story to tell or not and within an hour I was able to confirm that I was interested in acting as the ghost writer for his book.

I pitched the idea to my publisher at the time, Steve Caron at DB Publishing, and on 3 February was able to e-mail Tom to say we had a deal.

We agreed a 50/50 royalty split and met regularly to agree the structure for the book.

On 19 February we agreed a draft structure but importantly to me a timetable and a plan. Moxhull Hall Hotel became our regular meeting point and we decided to record Tom's thoughts, which I would then type up for Tom's approval or amendment. This was not my normal modus operandi as usually I hand-write my notes while listening to the subject talking and in hindsight I wish I had stayed with my regular approach as this record-and-write-up style inevitably resulted in virtually twice the work.

Our first meeting at Moxhull Hall was on 4 March and we were focussed on getting on to paper Tom's early life and influences in Birmingham. At that point we agreed to meet virtually every month so that we could track our progress against the plan. At this stage Tom was totally committed to the project and was keen to support it in as many ways as possible.

He had 700,000 listeners and more than 60,000 followers on Twitter, he had persuaded David Gold and Jasper Carrott to write forewords, he got a cartoonist pal to create a potential cover and provided me with an impressive list of sporting celebrities that would provide 'endorsements' on Tom and his work.

We worked hard through the year, meeting regularly and e-mailing content backwards and forwards to each other until we got to the end of October when the draft was up to 86,000 words and the project in my opinion had outgrown DB Publishing so I had managed to secure a deal in principle with my new publisher Pitch Publishing.

Pitch are much more proactive in terms of supporting authors via marketing, alternative book formats, launch dates, signings etc. but they were much more demanding in terms of meeting deadlines including the manuscript needing to be with them by the end of January 2016.

I worked hard to meet my self-imposed deadline of having a final draft available for our next meeting on 26 November at the Hotel Du Vin in Birmingham, a venue chosen to make it easier for Tom.

This was a critical meeting in our agreed timetable as we had a draft contract from Pitch to discuss. I had e-mailed the final draft to Tom on 5 November so that he could feed any changes back to me at this meeting. We agreed to meet and spend the morning taking the appropriate actions.

I sat in the hotel waiting for Tom and it was not until nearly 90 minutes after our appointment time that I received a text from him stating, 'I'm still at Villa, pal.'

It showed me that Tom had no respect for me or the process we were engaged in so I decided to immediately pull out of the project by replying to Tom via text, 'Forget it – the project not the appointment.'

I received no response from Tom but fortunately we were both at a Gala Events function at Warwickshire County Cricket Club and was therefore able to explain my decision and the reasons for it directly to him.

The following day I notified Pitch that I was no longer involved in the project and that in future they should talk to Tom directly. That didn't happen as Pitch said they were not interested if I was not involved.

Tom and I are still friends and his book was published on 1 August 2016 by DB Publishing. He was generous in his comments regarding my involvement in its production. In the introduction he writes, 'So at the tail end of my career and with the Independent Radio News (IRN) Gold award for "30 years outstanding service to radio" sitting proudly on a shelf at home I decided to speak with Keith Dixon, my initial ghost writer, to see if we could work on the book together – and here we are!'

In the acknowledgements he writes, 'To my initial co-writer, Keith Dixon, without whom I am sure I would never have had the discipline to sit down and put it all together in the first place and also for spending hours listening to my ramblings at Moxhull Hall Hotel. Keith is a prolific author and I can honestly say without his initial effort the book would never have happened. I can't thank you enough Keith.'

It is important as an author that you use yourself as a marketer for your books. You need to grow awareness of your book within your target market, which for me was easily identified as the supporters of Birmingham City Football Club.

Growing awareness is achieved in a number of ways:

1. Book reviews in magazines and newspapers
2. Book signings in retailers

3. Book sales area at related events
4. Radio and TV interviews
5. Special events

Let me give you an insight into some of my experiences related to growing the awareness of my books.

Book reviews in magazines and newspapers

To get a review is only possible if you donate a book to the publication and that does not guarantee coverage. The best coverage I got in newspapers was in the *Birmingham Mail* for Gil Merrick and the *Birmingham Post* for *50 Greatest Matches*. What happens of course is that the reporter uses some of the content of the book to fill his space in the publication and then gives you a credit at the end.

For Gil Merrick, the *Mail* reporter said, 'The book priced £16.99, *Gil Merrick*, is available now to buy in all good book shops.' For *50 Greatest Matches*, Andy Walker, who went on to be media and communications manager at St Andrew's and currently is providing the same function for the FA, gave me a two-page spread which featured five of the games featured in the book, and signed off with, '*Birmingham City – 50 Greatest Matches* by Keith Dixon is priced at £14.99 and is available now in all good book shops and on-line retailers. A stocking filler.' Well, it was December 2011.

Two football magazines have been supportive in providing reviews; *Late Tackle* and *BackPass*. Issue 14 of *BackPass*, for Christmas/New Year 2010/11, reviewed the Jackie Sewell book as follows, 'Cumberland-born Jackie Sewell was one of the most prolific inside-forward of the 1950s. He scored 228 League goals for Notts County, Sheffield Wednesday (who paid a world record £34,500 for him in 1951), Aston Villa and Hull City. Wearing his favourite No.8 shirt, Sewell helped Villa overcome Manchester United 2-1 in the 1957 FA Cup final. Peter McParland (who netted both Villa goals that day at Wembley) pays tribute to his old team-mate in the foreword.

'Sewell played for England on six occasions, netting three goals, one of them against Hungary in that infamous 6-3 drubbing at Wembley in 1953. After a less than happy spell at Boothferry Park, Sewell went on to enjoy an Indian summer in Africa, where he pioneered football (and initiated coaching programmes) in Rhodesia, Northern Rhodesia and the Belgian Congo. Sewell didn't hang up his boots until he was 46 and his great love of the game is very apparent from the in-depth interviews with him (he is now 83) that form the greater slice of this very decent biography (DP).'

A pretty good review and at least you get the impression that DP had read the book, which is not always the case as evidenced by this review for *The Leaders* in *BackPass* issue 47 (November and December 2015), 'This is the history of the most successful captains in the history of the West Midlands club, as defined by author Keith Dixon's criteria, which includes League Cup wins, FA Cup final appearances, successful promotion campaigns and Football League Trophy wins. The 15 skippers Dixon identified as worthy of this spotlight range from Ned Barkas, whose team reached the FA Cup Final in 1931, to Stephen Carr, who wore the armband as the Blues famously overturned Arsenal in the 2011 Carling Cup Final. There is a chapter, too, on the three players – Arthur Turner, Garry Pendrey and Steve Bruce – who have represented the club as captain and manager, and another on the current captain, Paul Robinson.'

Obviously I was grateful for the exposure but it got the title wrong by changing 'Official' into 'Original'!

Late Tackle is tougher with its reviews as it scores your book on a scale of one to ten but it does include a colour photograph of the cover. *The Leaders* got seven out of ten in issue 34 (December/January 2015). The reviewer Steven

Cooney had clearly read the book and made the following sign-off, 'Dixon has done a great job of breaking up the fascinating information with statistics and photos of mainly squad pictures, programmes and match report from the big games…It's an easy read that will appeal to Birmingham fans both young and old that maybe want to take a trip down memory lane or expand their knowledge – a fantastic addition to any Bluenose's Christmas stocking!'

Robbo – Unsung Hero got six out of ten in issue 30 (June/July 2015). John Lyons gave me this finish, 'What does come across very well in this book is Robinson's love of the game and determination, probably why he has had such a lengthy career in the top two divisions. All in all, this book isn't going to win any awards, but if you like Paul Robinson or the clubs he has played for, then this will have something for you. It's a decent, solid book, much like Robinson in many ways – and at times there's nothing wrong with that.'

With reviews it is very much a case of you put yourself and your work out there for assessment and you have to take it, good or bad. It is also great to get reviews from unexpected areas. In the fanzine *The Zulu* for the Blackpool fixture on 23 October 2010, Dave Small writes regarding Gil Merrick, 'I bought a copy and couldn't put it down until I'd read it from cover to cover. It's a brilliant book, it gives you an insight into the man giving many stories of many games, including the 1956 FA Cup Final, in particular his reasons why we lost.'

Book signings in retailers

Paul Robinson and I did two signings on 18 May 2015 at the Birmingham branches of Waterstone's and WH Smith. These events are publicised in-store and therefore the number of people attending is an unknown but both signings generated decent sales and provided Paul with great feedback as to how well respected he is by Midlands football fans.

We also had a great turnout when we officially launched his biography at the St Andrew's Superstore on 8 April 2015 prior to a Junior Blues event. Colin Tattum did a great job in spreading the word and we had representatives of Free Radio 80, Big Centre TV and the *Birmingham Mail* attending the event. They all carried subsequent coverage. The signing was also featured in the following Saturday's matchday programme.

Derby Books arranged a book signing event on Thursday 11 November 2010 at WH Smith in the Fort Shopping Centre in Birmingham which was entitled 'Local History and Sport'. Seven books were being promoted; three local history books, together with my releases, *Jackie Sewell* and *50 Greatest Matches*. Simon Goodyear was there with Gerry Hitchens and Bobby Thomson's book.

We were all set up in the ground floor entrance area of the store; Simon and myself together with Malcolm Page. Suddenly Bobby tore into the shop clearly in a rage which resulted in him chasing Simon up the escalator shouting that he was 'going to do' him. Later when things calmed down it seemed that Bobby thought that Simon was ripping him off regarding the sale of signed copies of his book. Thank goodness I was out of the firing line!

A much more sedate event was when Gil attended a signing event at WH Smith in Mell Square on the day of the Preston North End match when BCFC officially opened The Gil Merrick Stand. Gil was amazed at the number of people who were there to see him. They had positioned us in the book department on the first floor and people were queuing from the front door to see the great man.

Book sales area at related events
If you want to increase sales you have to be at related events and I have been to quite a few in my time. The Redditch

branch of the Blues supporters' club has invited me on a number of occasions to its regular Monday night meetings at the Oast Mill in Redditch. As a thank you to them I take along with me a celebrity player who is someway related to the subject of the book. They are always great nights as Paul Robinson, Jeff Kenna and Robert Hopkins can give testimony. Lynda and Peter Courts, thank you so much.

Matchdays at the Royal George Hotel in Tilton Road are something special and the McGroathys have been most generous in enabling me to have signing sessions before and after home games. Again I like to get players to join me and they are always well received as Jerry Gill, Tommy Mooney and Robert Hopkins can testify.

I have been lucky enough to be offered sales areas at BCFC organised events such as the following nights in 2015: Gary Rowett, Bob Latchford, Player of the Year awards and 140th Anniversary event. Four well-attended nights resulted in sales of 14 books!

Radio/TV interviews

I have been lucky to get radio interviews with Paul Franks, Tony Butler, Mark Regan and Tom Ross on local radio. National radio had eluded me until I managed to make contact with a producer at talkSPORT called John Cadigan who looked after the afternoon programme *Hawksbee and Jacobs*. John was interested in getting Paul Robinson into the studio to talk about the book but also to participate in a regular Friday afternoon feature about forecasting the football results for the upcoming weekend.

Paul and I attended talkSPORT's offices in London on Friday 22 May 2015 and settled in the green room with Matt Holland and Darren Gough. The original idea from John was that Paul and I would go into the studio but at the last minute I was told that I was surplus to requirements and only

Paul needed to be involved. I was surprised but didn't mind as we were getting national radio coverage which would only increase sales.

Paul also did a radio interview for Tom Ross's nightly football programme on Free Radio 80. It was on Monday 22 April 2015 and Tom's regular guest was Ian Taylor. At the end of the interview Paul was asked about how he felt about our book and he replied, 'I'm really pleased with the book and really pleased I got to work with Keith and talk to him about football. The way it was written was fantastic and we had great laughs doing it, so I am really pleased and I'm hoping that people, when they read it, enjoy it as well.'

After the Robbo book launch I was asked to do an interview for Big Centre TV by its sports producer Gary James. We did a live television interview in one of the corporate boxes at Edgbaston on 15 June 2016.

Special events

On 11 May 2014 I organised the official launch of *The Leaders* at my local pub, The Black Horse. I got great support from Paul Robinson, Malcolm Page and Ian Clarkson who attended the event and contributed to a question-and-answer session as well as signing autographs for the 24 guests I had in attendance.

Others

Books are always required for raffles, auctions and competitions and as an author you have to be prepared to invest time and books to help grow awareness of your products.

BCFC has been great in supporting my efforts which culminated in a meeting on 13 March 2015 with Ian Dutton, Wayne Cowen (superstore manager) and Colin Tattum at St Andrew's when I was granted the option to sub-title *The*

Leaders as the official publication for the 140th anniversary of the formation of BCFC. As you can imagine, I felt honoured to be given this authorisation, which was based on my track record as an author.

The ultimate measure of a book's success is how many copies are sold and in the past your only measure of 'success' was the size of your royalty cheque but today we have Amazon.

On 15 November 2016 Amazon UK quoted that it had available on its website 13.4m hardcover books, 34.7m paperbacks, 500,000 audiobooks and 4.9m Kindle publications, giving a total of 53.6m books!

Amazon also give each listed book an Amazon Best Sellers Rank, and while it is not that easy to understand how these rankings are calculated they do give an author some indication of how his titles are performing in the context of an overall availability of nearly 54m options.

At the time of writing my rankings are:

Title	In Books	In Biography – Sport – Football	In Sports, Hobbies etc. – Football	In Books – Sport – Football – British – Clubs	In Books – Sport – Football Club	In Books – Sport – Football Club – Aston Villa
Merrick	1,039,760	2,354	6,692			
Robbo	503,710	1,416	3,763			
Sewell	753,724	1,926	5,290			
50	1,745,184			2,894	3,035	
Heroes	1,798,154			2,960	3,035	
Leaders	484,693			1,070	1,096	
Bad Blood	522,007				1,166	23

What a great way to end this chapter. My book *Bad Blood* is number 23 in the top-selling 100 Aston Villa books chart on Amazon.

12

In the Press

Birmingham Post, Monday 30 April 2007
'We're bursting with pride after £40m promotion'
By Emma Brady

EXACTLY A year to the day since Birmingham City were relegated from football's top flight, they bounced back up to the Premiership – and a predicted windfall of £40 million.

Fans were jubilant as Blues beat Sheffield Wednesday 2-0 at St Andrew's on Saturday, many choked with emotion as their voices united to sing the club's anthem Keep Right On as the team took a lap of honour around the pitch.

But the celebrations began in earnest after promotion rivals Derby lost to Crystal Palace yesterday giving the Blues guaranteed entry to the Premiership next season.

Last night, managing director Karren Brady confirmed the cash, the result of a new television rights deal, would be used to strengthen the squad. 'Will there be funds for Steve Bruce to strengthen? Of course there will be,' she told the club's website. 'There is a lot of money coming into football next year from the broadcasting deal. Both Steve and myself, and the rest of the board, have learnt that once you get into the Premiership it is the only place to be, the only party to be at. We have learnt from our mistakes, we understand what needs to be done and that is going to take an enormous amount of investment. The board has got to stump that money up and has got to invest that money in the club's future.'

As the final whistle blew at Crystal Palace yesterday, Blues fans relaxed as they realised their place in the Premiership had been secured.

Keith Dixon, who founded the Bluenose Executive Club in 2002, said the crowd at St Andrew's on Saturday gave manager Bruce a standing ovation as he joined the team on a lap of honour.

The semi-retired director of Sleepy [Emma's error not mine] Magna, Warwickshire, who has been a Blues fan since 1954, said like most supporters he had got used to celebrating 'smaller victories'. He was at Saturday's match and told how, when striker Sebastian Larsson scored the second goal against Wednesday, 'everyone seemed to stop for a minute'.

Mr Dixon, aged 60, added, 'As a fan you always have to have faith, and we had a fantastic start to the season, but it was upsetting to lose that big lead we'd built up by Christmas. That said I never doubted that we'd go back up to the Premiership. It's where we belong. But when Larsson scored that second goal and all the team piled on top of him, everyone seemed to stop for a minute. It was like being frozen in time. It can be tough being a Birmingham City fan because we never seem to do things the easy way. We've been promoted upwards before, but we tend to celebrate the smaller victories, like beating Villa. Something always happens to us in these situations, and on Saturday when Fabrice Muamba was sent off and Wednesday's best attempt hit the crossbar, it seemed to transform our ten-men team.'

Mr Dixon, who was eight when he first went to St Andrew's, also believes Blues will flourish in the

Premiership and is confident they will not be returning to the Championship any time soon. He said: 'This is the season to go up because the Sky payment is something like £40 million or £50 million, and I think the parachute money is the same as well. Steve Bruce has completely changed the team, it's full of enthusiastic young players who will continue to get better. I think next season will be tough, it'll definitely be another roller coaster, but I'm confident we'll stay up next season.' He added: 'My son is actually a Man Utd fan, so we say he's a Red Devil with a Bluenose, but if he thinks we'll be an easy three points for them next season he could be in for a surprise.'

Birmingham Evening Mail 3 June 2008 – Your Shout – fans have their say

'Fans let down by Blues board'

I am writing in response to the article by Martin O'Connor (*Mail* May 29 and letter from C. Cotter of Yardley)

In my opinion the Blues' board do care about the club but have the unhappy knack of shooting themselves in the foot by not giving sufficient thought to the implications of their actions or comments, which alienate most of the hardcore Blues supporters. Is my opinion valid? Well my credentials are that I have supported Blues since the age of eight, 53 years in total.

When I was MD of Triton Showers I convinced the board to sponsor Blues for three years and I founded the Bluenose Club which has generated income for various charities through the connection with ex-players, the fans and, on one occasion, with the support of David Gold.

In 1992 the club was run by the Kumars who 'played a bit themselves' but had no cash and tried to run the club like the market traders they were. David Sullivan saved the club by buying it from the Receivers, Leonard Curtis. While there was a lot of interest from local business people at the time, not one put forward an acceptable offer. How do I know this? Because I have the original handwritten diary of the receivership from Monday November 1 1992 until the deal was ratified on Saturday March 6 1993. There was no Brummie benefactor out there.

Because of the working-class nature of the Bluenose 'caring enough to save our club' brought David Sullivan and his team enormous collateral in terms of respect. Since then they have eroded the value of this collateral in a number of ways:

1. Messing up on a regular basis the sales of season tickets (Cotter's letter refers to this) and associated discounts
2. Complaining about poor attendances when they have sold the TV rights for the game
3. Championing their commitment to the club by saying they travel two hours plus for every home game. Most of us do that but not in the back of a chauffeur-driven limo. Try sitting on the Coventry Road or Bordesley Green East bus after matches. (Note: Sullivan says: *'There are no home games for me and it can be depressing to be stuck on the M1 when you are trying to get home to see your children before they go to bed'*)
4. Justifying ticket prices by comparing the cost to a London West End show. You get guaranteed quality in the West End for £35 – unlike St Andrew's
5. Dismissing the financials related to a big-screen facility protesting it would lose money and they 'want every penny to go to players'. Every penny? In the accounts for year ending August 2007, Roldvale were paid £485,000 for David Sullivan's time, the Golds' company got the same fees and Sports Newspapers got £52,000 for the loan of their finance director. Exhorbitant sums for non-executive contributions.

The current Blues board will never get the loyalty it arguably deserves if it continues to treat the fans with such disdain.

K. Dixon Sheepy Magna

My wife, Julie has often said that I get as much pleasure from the Villa losing as I do the Blues winning. This is patently not true, but to see the Villa relegated to the Championship gave me such pleasure that I had to record it for posterity and therefore submitted an article to *Late Tackle* which appears below.

Late Tackle magazine article issue 37 May/June 2016
'Villa's great season – for a Bluenose'
Birmingham City fan Keith Dixon admits Aston Villa's desperate season has provided bundles of laughs….

In Birmingham at the moment there is great concern within the media and associated football communities about the demise of Aston Villa. The fact that this 'great' club could lose its Premier League membership, which it has held since the formation of the league in 1992, seems too much to bear for the local community and the Villa fans.

Villa seem certain to lose their annual relegation battle this time around, American owner Randy Lerner guiding them to the second tier. Perhaps Villa fans should have been alerted to the limit of their club's ambitions for 2015/16 when Christian Benteke (£32.5m to Liverpool) and Fabian Delph (£8m to Manchester City) were sold last summer and replaced with unknown foreign players with no experience of English football let alone the Premier League and a potential relegation dogfight.

And with things looking bleak in the new year, there wasn't much comfort for the fans when the January transfer window closed with no business done.

While one half of England's second city is in mourning, the fans of Birmingham City are virtually ecstatic or as my wife would say, 'You get as much pleasure from the Villa losing as you do from the Blues winning.'

It's not the 4-0 defeat to Manchester City or the 6-0 humiliation at home to Liverpool that gives the Bluenoses the most pleasure, it's the way the fans, the club and the media find it so difficult to accept the disappointments.

The problem for Villa is that they believe their own publicity. They believe, totally erroneously, that they are a 'great' club, endorsed in some way by the media referring to their European Cup victory whenever the opportunity arises. So what does the future hold for Villa? Well, I fear things could get a lot worse.

After Birmingham were relegated from the Premier League in 2011, the majority of our squad were shipped out to cut the wage bill. At least we had players that were worthy of top division status. Is that the case at Villa Park? I think not. They could be lumbered with a lot of players on hefty contracts. Perhaps a few transfer fees will come their way, but there aren't too many top-class players there. Okay, they'll receive parachute payments, though Birmingham City saw very little of those income streams – the money drifted to the other side of the world.

Paul Lambert, Tim Sherwood and Remi Garde failed to produce performances on the pitch that at least gave the Villa fans hope. I believe a factor in their inability to create a team of players that will give their all for the jersey is the lack of connection at the club.

I have sat with my son and watched my team lose 8-0 at home to Bournemouth. While we were well beaten, the players never gave up.

We have appointed an ex-player who took virtually the same group of players and gave us respectability before, this season, leading us to a league position just outside the play-offs (at the time of writing). Manager Gary Rowett joined in October 2014, bringing with him a further two ex-Blues in the form of Mark Sale and Kevin Summerfield as part of his coaching team.

St Andrew's has returned to the status of a fortress, we get a regular attendance of around 18,000 and our away allocation is always sold out.

Believe me, Villa will find it incredibly difficult to adapt to life in the Championship. It's a rough and tumble league where their failed aristocrats will have to fight for every ball and every point.

It delights me to say I think they will struggle in the Championship but at least we are guaranteed six points next season, unless we get promoted!

That would be a dream come true, Blues in the Premier League and Villa in the Championship!

I cannot bring myself to join in with the Tilton Road end's chant to 'Sh*t on the Villa'. However, although I am 69 and should know better, I delight in the Villa's downfall.

My original submission is reproduced below. Major omissions are interesting and highlighted:

In Birmingham at the moment there is great concern within the media and associated football communities about the demise of Aston Villa. The fact that this 'great' club could lose its Premier League membership, which it has held since the formation of the league in 1992 seems too much to bear for the local community and the Villa fans.

Apparently the club has been mismanaged for nearly five years with annual relegation escapes a symptom of the disease, which manifests itself as the club's American owner Randy Lerner, who has openly had the club 'up for sale' for at least two years with no serious interest expressed.

Perhaps Villa fans should have been alerted to the limit of their club's ambitions for 2015/16 when Benteke and Delph were sold at 'below market' transfer fees and replaced with unknown foreign players with no experience of English football let alone the Premier League and a potential relegation dog fight.

Not much comfort for the fans when the January transfer window closed with no business transacted but at least Randy appointed a new chairman from KPMG, a non-executive director who used to run the Bank of England, and sacked the club's financial director but retained the world-famous French-speaking Remi Garde.

While one half of England's second city is in mourning, the fans of Birmingham City are virtually ecstatic or as my wife would say, 'You get as much pleasure from the Villa losing as you do from the Blues winning.'

It's not the 4-0 defeat away to Manchester City or the 6-0 humiliation at home to Liverpool that gives the Bluenoses pleasure but it's the way the fans, the club and the media find it so difficult to accept the disappointments of being a football club.

The problem for Villa is that they believe their own publicity and believe totally erroneously that they are a 'great' club, endorsed in some way by the media referring to their European Cup victory whenever the opportunity arises.

While the focus is on Aston, a suburb of Birmingham, the Rowett revolution at Birmingham City is virtually ignored by the media, yet I believe it indicates the future for our near neighbours.

> Foreign owners do not understand English football whether they are American or Chinese but they are the future and the potential growth of Chinese involvement in the game throughout the world is scary. This is not xenophobia or anti-Chinese; it is based on experience as the Blues are owned by an ex-hairdresser who is a convicted criminal, who appointed a chief executive who reportedly had links with the Hong Kong criminal fraternity, and lost all interest in the club when we were relegated from the Premier League after beating Arsenal in the Carling Cup Final in 2011.
>
> The reason he purchased my club was to launder some money and expand his media rights and sportswear businesses, the latter two made impossible when our status was reduced to the Championship.
>
> We are now under the control of Baker Tilly in Hong Kong who were appointed by the shareholders when the acrimony between Yeung and Pannu threatened to destroy all corporate governance within Birmingham International Holdings, whose only reason for not selling Birmingham City Football Club is that they need a trading company to enable it to retain its membership of the Hong Kong stock exchange. This is evidenced by Baker Tilley awarding an unprecedented two and a half years exclusivity period for Trillion Trophy of Asia to produce an acceptable offer for the Blues.

So beware Villa fans as to whom Lerner sells the club. It could get a lot worse, mark my words.

After Birmingham were relegated from the Premier League in 2011 the majority of our squad were shipped out to cut the salary bill, at least we had players that were worthy of top division status – is that the case at Villa Park, I think not and therefore hefty playing contracts will deplete the revenues obtainable in the Championship and thereby reduce investment in the attempt to regain Premier League status.

Hopefully Villa will benefit from any transfer fees obtained plus the guaranteed parachute payments, Birmingham City saw very little of the above income streams as the money drifted to the other side of the world.

Lambert, Sherwood and Garde have failed to produce performances on the pitch that at least give the Villa fans hope. I believe a factor in their inability to create a team of players that will give their all for the club, is the lack of connection with the football club.

I have sat with my son and watched my team lose 8-0 at home to Bournemouth and while we were well beaten the players never gave up. We then appointed an ex-player who took virtually the same group of players and gave us respectability before leading us to a league position just outside the play-offs (at the time of writing). Gary Rowett joined in October 2014 bringing with him a further two ex-Blues players in the form of Mark Sale and Kevin Summerfield as part of his coaching team.

St Andrew's has returned to the status of 'a fortress', we get a regular attendance of around 18,000 and our away allocation is always 'sold out'.

Villa will find it incredibly difficult to adapt to life in the Championship, it's a 'rough and tumble' league where the Villa failed 'aristocrats' will have to fight for every ball and every point. It delights me to say I think they will struggle in the Championship but at least we are guaranteed six points next season, unless we get promoted!

That would be a dream come true, Blues in the Premier League and Villa in the Championship!

Although I am 69 and should know better I delight in the Villa's downfall. Having said that I cannot bring myself to join in with the Tilton's chant to 'Sh*t on the Villa'.

Blues magazine – March 2008 issue 43
Keith Dixon, one of the *Blues* magazine columnists, has put together his own 12 point plan...

My 12 point plan to save the beautiful game

1. Restructure Players' Pay

If a player is worth £50,000 a week to a club then that's their business but as results impact on the club's future in so many ways, surely it's sensible to restructure that £50,000 such that it includes a performance-related element. What's wrong with a basic salary of £30,000 plus with a win bonus of £20,000 and a draw bonus of £10,000? If the team loses, the player only gets their basic £30,000. Will this not create a more competitive performance on the pitch from every player and a better spectacle for the fans?

2. Restrict Foreign Players

There should be an agreed maximum percentage of foreign players in a club's overall playing staff. This would enable more home grown players to get a greater opportunity of first team football.

3. No points for 0-0 draw

At the beginning of a game the score is 0-0 so why do we encourage defensive play by giving one point to each team for achieving 'nothing' in 90 minutes? It should be three points for a win and two points for a scoring draw. Nothing for a goalless game.

4. Scrap Play-Offs

Everyone in football complains about the number of games played and the length of the season so let's scrap the meaningless play-offs. Any side that has finished third in the Championship deserves promotion!

5. Juniors for £5

The future of football is, as with all things, in the hands of our children. Parents with youngsters cannot easily afford the cost of going to a game so they consider other options for the Saturday afternoon entertainment. Every club should charge £5 for juniors and £10 for an accompanying adult for all home games.

6. Re-introduce Schools Football

The current Academy system is too 'middle-class'. How many working-class parents can get their sons to Academies for an early evening training session twice a week and to games at the weekend? TV money should be used to introduce a structured schools football coaching system supported by a local professional club. This would ensure that all interested children get the chance to learn the game at the earliest opportunity and talented players get identified.

7. Premier Clubs 'Twinning' With Lower Division Clubs

Formal 'twinning' relationships should be created by top clubs with their local lower league neighbours, thereby strengthening the smaller club in a number of ways e.g.

marketing support, coaching support, player support. Young professionals from the Premier club could be 'loaned' to gain first-team experience for a complete season with their wages paid by the Premier club.

8. Bring Back Terraces
Limited standing areas should be introduced to grounds. All-seater stadiums restrict atmosphere and this is shown at every game because when the game gets exciting what do we do? We stand up briefly and the whole atmosphere in the ground changes!

9. Introduce 'Rolling' Substitutes
Let's see how tactically aware our managers are! They have five substitutes on the bench so what's wrong with bringing a sub on for ten minutes immediately to achieve a specific short-term objective and then taking him off again when the job is done!

10. Scrap 'Extra Time'
Extra time in cup competitions has become sterile and a complete waste of 30 minutes as very rarely do teams use that period to get a result. The penalty shootout, which we know is not ideal, let's go to that immediately after 90 minutes.

11. Football Journalism Restricted to Facts Only
There is so much hype in football that has little positive effect on the game. How much better our back pages would be if the journalists gave us real news based on actual fact!

12. Every Board to Include a Representative of the Fans
No tokenism. But a long-term fan is invited to attend

board meetings and make a contribution to the decision-making of the club.

On 22 December 2016 I submitted the following to John Lyons, editor of *Late Tackle*:

A FAN IN THE BOARDROOM? ONLY FOR CIRCULATING AIR!

In October 2014 the Labour party unveiled its plans to give football fans a voice in every boardroom and buy a significant slice of the shares when the ownership of their club changed.

It was a headline-grabbing statement that was clearly a device to raise the profile of the party together with an attempt to increase membership numbers as well as testing the water to see what response their plans might evoke.

To date there has been very little positive response to the plans other than it is a thought-provoking, well-constructed idea but with very little hope of successful implementation.

The concept of having a fan actively participating in the club is not a new one and has never achieved wide acceptance, even when football clubs were owned and managed by local people who understood the game, the club and its heritage and its importance to the neighbouring community. If it didn't happen then it will not happen in the 21st century when clubs are largely owned and managed by foreigners who are only interested in the club as a business and a vehicle to promote their football brand to the vast markets of the Far East and America.

Look at the changes which have occurred in the boardroom of my club, Birmingham City.

In the early 90s the club was unsuccessfully run by an Indian family who understood the clothing industry but not football, it was then sold to David Sullivan, a businessman in the newspaper industry, who turned the club's fortunes around such that he sold it to Carson Yeung for in excess of £80m, not a bad return on an initial investment of £600,000 for 84 per cent of the shareholding.

Sullivan moved on to home territory when he bought West Ham United but even he and David Gold as Hammers fans chose profit over heritage when the chance to move from Boleyn Road presented itself.

In late 2016 Trillion Trophy Asia has bought Birmingham City and installed four Chinese directors and one Greek director to run the club with the curious promise not to sell the club for a period of two years.

During these 25 years the St Andrew's boardroom has had no one in a decision-making role who understood the local community, the game and the club's history.

As a fan you can witness the erosion of these vital connections and often it is to the club's ultimate detriment both on and off the field of play.

Labour's plan was drawn up in consultation with 95 football supporters' organisations and requires supporters to form a single accredited trust in return for the right to appoint and remove directors and purchase shares. This, Labour says, will ensure that those running clubs must share information, power and responsibility with the fans. Do Labour really believe in its wildest dreams that directors and shareholders will allow outsiders to contribute to the decision-making that will affect the growth of their business in which they have invested their cash and time?

Imagine the directors of Marks and Spencer appointing one of its customers to the board to participate in pricing, products, store acquisition etc. Although the customer will have the welfare of the business at heart, they simply will not have the required skills to make a positive contribution at the most senior level of management.

Again it's a nice idea but totally impractical.

Workers' representation on boards has been tried in the past and all that it created is a two-tier board system; one of which makes decisions and the other is a sounding-board for ideas and suggestions. Guess which one the workers' representative attended.

The plan talks about the lack of accountability at clubs which has led to clubs being relocated away from fan-bases, debt and insolvency and high ticket prices. No one can disagree with that but fans in the boardroom will have no positive impact on resolving those very real issues.

There seems to be a misunderstanding that football club boardrooms are full of directors who do not care, are only interested in themselves and are determined to drive their clubs into financial disarray. This simply is not the case and while the recent boardroom history at St Andrew's has been chequered most of its occupants have had the best interests of the club at heart, with the possible exception of the money-laundering Carson Yeung.

I spend the majority of my working life on the boards of several UK companies in the capacity of a non-executive director/chairman. My role is to ensure the company operates with financial probity, within corporate governance guidelines and looks to protect the interests of all the company's stakeholders which are its customers, suppliers, shareholders and employees. Alongside these responsibilities I have to support the business in its growth strategy and business planning.

Unless a football fan can contribute in these challenging areas then they will not be welcome in any boardroom. Labour's plan suggests the new organisation will provide training to fan directors and knowledge is one thing but a director's value comes from knowledge and experience, it is not something that can be learnt.

The lack of appetite for a fan presence in the boardroom is clearly evidenced by my own experience at Birmingham City where I have offered my services as a non-executive director on a free-of-charge basis.

My credentials? A fan for 62 years who has held senior executive board positions since 1984 and been a non-executive director since 1996. The response I received was a resounding 'No, thanks'.

Of course I am disappointed but my main emotion, as both a fan and a businessman, is one of concern because there is massive antipathy to the current Chinese ownership of football clubs in Birmingham and the West Midlands and elsewhere and unless the club's boards of directors do something positive to reduce this negativity and improve relationships between the clubs and their supporters then football is on a difficult road, one which will lead to smaller crowds, lower revenues and reduced sponsorship opportunities, all of which will make achieving the club's financial forecasts difficult if not impossible.

This is an outcome that would not be welcomed in any football club boardroom and would not be improved by having a token fan on the board.

On 14 February 2017 I sent the following article to John Lyons... I titled it 'New Direction?' but when it was published in issue 44 March/April 2017 it had been retitled 'Feeling Blue'.

It's Valentine's Day 2017 and Birmingham City fans are heading for Preston North End to witness Gianfanco Zola's 13th game in charge of our beloved Blues.

When Gary Rowett and his team were sacked with immediate effect in December 2016 it was a major shock to all Bluenoses but a greater shock was awaiting us when the news broke that Rowett had been replaced by Zola, a great player but a manager/coach with no track record of success.

At the time of Rowett's sacking Birmingham City were seventh in the Championship and optimism was being felt all around St Andrew's. It is true to say that Rowett always set his teams up, not to lose but with limited funds and a team of free transfer and loan players the general feeling was that we were punching above our weight. So what was the thinking behind the change?

The official club statement on 14 December gave little clues other than, 'However, new owners Trillion Trophy Asia (TTAL) remains determined to lead the club to a bright and exciting future. Supporters can rest assured that the decision has been taken with a strategic, long-term view and with the club's best interests at heart. Club director Panos Pavlakis, on behalf of the board, said, "I would ask that all our supporters trust our judgement and look forward to and embrace the future as we begin to implement the exciting vision of TTAL."

On the day of the appointment of Zola, Panos said on the official website, 'We are delighted to welcome Gianfranco and his backroom team to the club. His pedigree, philosophy and ambition fits with what we like to achieve as we move in a new direction.'

So that's it, BCFC are moving in a 'new direction'. Is that the same direction that Panos revealed on 7 June 2016 at the launch of the new Adidas kit and new sponsor 888 Sport? He was quoted in the *Birmingham Mail* at the Resorts World event, 'However one thing I can definitely say, after more than two years as Blues director, is that I truly feel and believe that this [the takeover by TTAL which had not been completed at this time] is one of the most important and significant steps for BCFC which could lead us further to the right direction. This is the direction that will bring a steady, strong but always honest team ready to progress back where we belong. The Future is Blue.'

So the changes since June 2016 to today have all been about moving in a 'new direction'.

The evidence so far is mixed.

Currently we are 12th in the Championship, after 13 games Zola has won one game and the Blues have scored fewer goals than any other side in the division – six goals in ten games and over half of them have been scored by Lukas Jutkiewicz who was signed by Rowett.

Let me make it clear I am not a Rowett fan, I am simply recording the facts as it is obviously a factor regarding our results that our top goalscorer, Clayton Donaldson, has not played since Zola was appointed.

Although Zola's performance on the pitch has not been good there has been plenty of activity off the pitch. With funds released to him by TTAL he has secured the services of Jerome Sinclair, Krystian Bielik and Craig Gardner on loan until the end of the season while securing the permanent services of Dan Scarr, Emilio Nsue, Cheick Keita and Kerin Frei on long-term contracts.

While this has been going on Zola has removed four international players from our squad, Paul Caddis (Scotland), Jonathan Spector (USA), David Cotterill (Wales) as well as our Italian international Diego Fabbrini. I have not taken my tongue out of my cheek but on a serious note let's explore Zola's 'pedigree' as described by Panos. There is no doubt that Zola was a magnificent player scoring 193 goals in a career that amassed 627 games.

2 July 2006 to 10 September 2008 – assistant head coach to Italy national under-21 team which reached the quarter-finals of the 2008 Olympic Games in Bejing.

10 September 2008 to 11 May 2010 – appointed manager of West Ham United despite not having the required UEFA

A Licence – he was sacked at the end of 2009/10 with West Ham in 17th place five points above relegation.

7 July 2012 to 16 December 2013 – in his first season as Watford manager, the club finished third and made the play-offs – he resigned with the club 13th in the league without a win since October 2013 and having lost their last five games.

26 December 2014 to 9 March 2015 – appointed head coach of Cagliari and after less than three months he was sacked and the club was relegated.

6 July 2015 to 27 June 2016 – appointed head coach of Al Arabi in the Qatar Stars league, he was sacked after one season with his team winning ten games out of 26, losing 11 and finishing eighth in a league of 14.

Certainly a pedigree to excite the imagination of all Blues fans?

The biggest issue for me is that BCFC are trading in a business which can only sell to its supporters, providing a product which offers no guarantee of quality to its customers. It asks its loyal customers to pay upfront for this product and to make the product even less desirable, the date of delivery can be changed without any consideration of its customers' reaction based on the interests of an unrelated third party. No other industry would operate in this way as it is a business model which can only lead to failure in financial terms.

Only football and its clubs operate as above and that is because the flawed business model described previously is underpinned by the broadcasting revenues. Let's face it, the Premier League clubs do not require fans to attend their matches for them to be profitable. Fans are merely a backdrop to a television programme. It is my opinion that this state of affairs is unsustainable in the medium to long term because as Gary Rowett was quoted after his sacking, 'Like I said before if you own a football club you have a right to do whatever you want, people don't have to be happy, fans don't have to be happy, the football world doesn't have to be happy. But that is ultimately your choice to go in whatever direction you chose and good luck to Birmingham.'

I think we are going to need it.

13

Academy Scout

I WAS spending most of my weekends in the early 2000s watching my son Harry playing for teams in the north Warwickshire and south Staffordshire junior leagues. I then saw an advertisement on the club's website regarding vacancies for scouts.

After applying I had to obtain an Enhanced Criminal Record Certificate before the club was able to confirm my appointment. It was quite a thrill to see on the ECRC that I was an employee of Birmingham City Football Club. So from March 2004 until July 2007 I was looking for potential players for my beloved Blues.

I was appointed by Steve Hopcroft, the academy recruitment officer at the time, who was receiving between 100 and 150 letters a week from budding young stars all asking the same question, 'Can I join Blues' Academy?'

As an ex-scout himself he understood the task intimately and how vital the scouting system was to meeting his objective of attracting the best players in the under-9 to under-16 age groups to Wast Hills.

His view was, 'I have lots of scouts working for us but it's difficult because there are thousands of boys out there, all wanting to be watched at the same time. We respond to every letter but I'll only send a scout to watch them if they're up to the age of 14 or 15, live within our area and have been a district or county player.'

The academy had a clear vision which was encompassed in the following statements within the recruitment manual 2006/07:

An environment that represents excellence

It demands high standards in all people and symbolises respect, hard work, commitment and honesty

A place to pursue success

Blues had invested heavily in the academy thanks to Trevor Francis and Brian Eastick, the academy manager. Brian had five departments under him; U7-U16; U17, U18, U19; Medical; Education; Support.

The scouts worked under the U7-U16 department.

All scouts had to work to a code of conduct which was:

- Be smart in appearance, appropriate to the occasion remembering they represent BCFC
- Carry club identification at all times
- To deal with team managers in a professional manner, introduce yourself showing your club identification, being respectful and polite
- Be sensitive to the time in which you approach a manager
- Communicate with parents/guardians in a professional and friendly manner
- Work in line with the academy child protection policy
- Be thorough in administration. Ensure you have all the details and ensure they are not currently at another club
- Ensure all information is passed on to the recruitment officer at the earliest opportunity

As scouts we were given clear guidelines as to what the club from first team to academy levels were looking for.

This was the statement from the document entitled 'An Aid to Scouting'.

'It is very important that we are all very selective when scouting and to identify players who have the necessary skills for them to be successful in academy football. To do this YOU must understand what WE expect of any player that is recommended for trial. We have all spoken about the importance of speed, athleticism, personality and technique. Once this has been established it is preferable if the player is tall, lean and quick. I cannot emphasise enough how important it is that you pay attention to these aspects of a player's make-up before you consider him as a potential trialist:

- Defenders must be competitive and quick
- Central defenders must be tall
- Midfield players must have excellent technique and have a good athletic ability
- Strikers must be quick and have an eye for a goal
- Remember if they cannot run they cannot trial no matter what position they play'

Where we went and what matches we watched was up to the scout but as well as adhering to the code of conduct we had to complete a scouting report for any player we considered met the above criteria and therefore was suitable for a trial.

We had to record date, venue, fixture, age group, player's position, player's name, date of birth and then fill in an analysis based on a one-to-ten ratio:

Athletic Ability/ Physical Size & Shape	Technical	Tactical Awareness	Temperament	Competitiveness

Key:
10/9 – Exceptional 8/7 – Trialist 6 – worth 2nd look 5/4 Average/below average 3/2/1 – Poor

We then had to print our name and sign the form. We were also encouraged to add comments.

A trial period was for a maximum of six consecutive weeks only. Players were not obliged to remain at the club on trial for six weeks and neither was the club obliged to keep the player on trial for the full six weeks – it was a maximum. Once a player attended a football academy his details were notified to the Football League by the club.

The player was required to attend training twice a week for sessions, which ran from 6.15pm to 8.15pm. Travelling times were restricted dependent on age, so for U9-U12 a player had to reside within one hour, while for U13-U16 it was increased by 30 minutes.

As scouts we got paid. When a player was registered the following forms had to be completed for the Football League:

U9, 10, 11 and 12	One Year	Form YD4	Scout paid £50
U13-14	Two Years	Form YD4	Scout paid £50
U13-U16	Four Years	Form YD6	Scout paid £200
U15-U16	Two Years	Form YD4	Scout paid £50
Registration of player on scholarship agreement			Scout paid £500
Registration of player on professional contract			Scout paid £1,000

During my period there I earned £50. My successful trialist was Lewis Mosley and my comments were:

'Lewis contacted the Academy directly requesting a trial and I was asked by Vic Callow to follow up his enquiry.

'I have watched "Mozza" three times: playing above his age group i.e. Under 15s in the Coventry League and twice for his Under 14 side in both Cup and League fixtures, and consider him worthy of being seen on trial at the Academy.

'Lewis also plays for the District side. He acts as captain for both club sides.

'He is extremely tall and strong for his age and while he currently plays a holding role in midfield I think his best position is as a central defender.'

On 20 November 2006 I received a letter from Mark Fogarty, the Academy recruitment officer at the time, which read:

> Dear Keith
> I would like to thank you for identifying and referring Lewis Mosley to Birmingham City Football Club Academy. I am delighted to inform you that he has now signed for the club on a one year contract. In view of this would you please complete the attached invoice and return it to me at your earliest convenience. Once again, congratulations and keep up the good work.

On 16 October 2006, the recently appointed Academy manager, Terry Westley wrote to me saying, 'I would like to take this opportunity to put in writing my sincere thanks for the support you have shown since my arrival at BCFC. I am extremely grateful for the contribution you make to this Academy, especially during the winter months when many cold Saturdays and Sundays see you standing on the sidelines of local park pitches but rest assured, your commitment and loyalty to Birmingham City FC is much appreciated. I look forward to catching up with you again during the coming months.'

Scouts Brian Umbers and Charlie Leaver were colleagues during my time and they were extremely helpful when I wanted to assess whether my son Harry was good enough for a trial. Obviously it is difficult not to be biased when it's your family. At that time Harry was playing for Atherstone

Rangers under-10s and after the nod from Charlie, he went on trial with the Blues on 27 April 2004. He played in two friendlies within his first two weeks against Halesowen Colts under-12s and Solihull Town under-11s. These games were eight-a-side and played in four phases of 20 minutes. On both occasions Harry played in two sections and scored against Solihull in a 6-5 defeat. His trial ended on 8 June with the conclusion by Jon O'Neill that he should 'be monitored for future progress'.

True to their word, Harry was invited back to check his progress on 12 March 2006 but regrettably, on 18 March he broke his arm playing against St John's for Atherstone Rangers under-12s. The club were great with his obvious disappointment and Steve Hopcroft confirmed that he would be back on trial in August after adherence to the club's policy that once the plaster is removed there would be a four-week non-contact period.

On 2 August his trial re-started under the coach Richard Beale (who at the time of writing is senior professional development coach) and was there for seven weeks before he had a meeting with one of the coaches, Kristjaan Speakman (who at the time of writing is Academy manager), on 13 September when he was told there would be no offer as he was slightly below standard on technique, which meant he was no better than the existing squad therefore he would not improve it. His plus points were his hard work, intelligence regarding positioning, enthusiasm, attention and application of the instructions he was given.

One strange thing about the coaching he received is that although he was a striker and dead ball specialist, during his time at Wast Hills he was never subject to either shooting or free-kick practice sessions.

My time as a scout ended when I received a letter from Mark Fogarty on 12 July 2007 which read:

BLUES INSIDER

Dear Keith

I would like to thank you for all your hard work last season. We have appointed a number of regional scouts, a new inner city scout, overseas scouts and elite scouts. If you wish to work as a spotter in one of our areas please call me and we will place you into the appropriate region.

However if you cannot get about to watch players as part of running a team then you will not be able to fit into the new role. If the latter is the case, please feel free to call me when you do spot a player in one of your games and we will be delighted to follow this up.

By this time Harry had been recruited into the under-15s of Tamworth Football Club and I felt that my time as a scout/spotter should come to an end.

14

Chinese Crackers

BEFORE STARTING to write this chapter I felt it was important to the reader to put some sort of timeline on the page to hopefully make this whole chapter in Blues' history a little clearer.

On 20 August 2009 Grandtop International placed a deposit of £3m ahead of a proposed takeover which was put back from October to mid-November because of a delay in the EGM required to approve the issue of an additional 50 per cent of shares following a £5m bridging loan to cover the purchase of the club. Final documents outlining Carson Yeung's £1-per-share offer was sent to shareholders in mid-September. By 24 September acceptances were received on 81.7 per cent of shares and by the closing date of 6 October the takeover was complete with acceptances at 94 per cent, a level allowing a compulsory purchase of the rest.

At a press conference on 15 December the board was announced as: Carson Yeung (president); Mike Wiseman (vice-president); Peter Pannu (chairman); Sammy Yu (vice-chairman); Michael Dunford (chief executive officer). Soon after that, Grandtop International became Birmingham International Holdings.

Prior to this Reuters reported on 15 September 2009 from Beijing, 'Hong Kong billionaire Carson Yeung, who hopes to complete his $130 million purchase of Birmingham City in the next three weeks, wants the Premier League club to spearhead a revolution in Chinese soccer.

'Yeung's Grandtop International Holdings Limited expected its bid to buy a controlling interest in the club to be approved by shareholders at a meeting on Sept. 29, he said.

'Emphasising that stability at the English club would be their initial watchword, Yeung also spoke of his vision of Birmingham helping to cure China's soccer ills. "Over the ten years China has had its sports boosted, but there has been no development for football," Yeung told a news conference on Tuesday.

'"So I would like to make my humble contribution. In the future when the team is stabilised, we will recruit Chinese players who have potential.

'"My biggest wish is to bring in the English Premier League club to China, promote English professionalism and football concepts to the Chinese, and to let the Chinese know how an English football team is managed."

'Carson Yeung arrived at St Andrew's on Thursday 15 October, some two years after he had bought a 29.9 per cent stake in the club. The Hong Kong businessman at a press conference promised to spend £80m in 2010 with 50 per cent of it available to Alex McLeish when the January transfer window opens. His company Grandtop International completed the £81.5m takeover of Birmingham City and Carson took on the role of president. Yeung, who failed with a takeover bid two years ago, is expected to oversee his first game as Birmingham's new owner against Arsenal on Saturday week. The priority is to stay in the Premier League with the ambition to be up there with Manchester United and Chelsea.

'New chairman Vic Hui believed that Birmingham City could follow in the footsteps of top basketball star Yao Ming, who played for Houston Rockets, and the NBA now earns £1.5bn a year from Chinese interest. At the time, Hui said, "We have very good connections in the China market. We have lots of opportunity to bring the Premier League concept to China and develop football. Later on I think we will have a China player at Birmingham. It's like the NBA – before Yao Ming I don't think a lot of Chinese people were watching NBA. The NBA market developed in China very, very fast. So there is a model. Other Premier League clubs have tried but our privilege is we're Chinese.

'"We know the way it works. From merchandising to the media, there are a lot of ways to make a profit. We could be the best supported club in the world. All enterprises are looking at the market in China now. The economy grows very fast. The people are more educated and looking for a better standard of life. So I think they will like the Premier League. I think we are taking two years. I can say everyone knows Birmingham because of Carson Yeung. I can't say we are more famous than Manchester United. But we have our privileged position."

'Yeung declared, "We will be looking for potential young players in China so that all Chinese people love Birmingham City as their favourite team. We will be more popular than Manchester United and Chelsea. We are confident, we have comrades, we have content and we will work together."

'Sammy Yu, Grandtop's chief operations officer, who used to manage the Hong Kong national team said, "I've been running around the training pitch with Alex. I will work closely with him because I have been involved in coaching and managing for 40 years so I can share some experience with him. The support to Alex is very important because, looking at the coaching and training staff, we look a bit short. But Alex makes the decisions and we totally support him. We will not be crazy buyers, spending crazy money for nothing.

'"In football, even if you spend a fortune, it doesn't mean you will succeed. We want to strengthen the club step-by-step. We have a lot of friends in football circles...with expertise in the Premier League, of even higher class than the existing management. We will work together with the current management. Mr Yeung will be the final decision-maker, but we need a team to run the club.

'Former England winger Steve McManaman and France midfielder Christian Karembeu were expected to help out, but probably in areas such as scouting and international relations. The mission to improve Chinese soccer would include building a dedicated school, inviting Chinese coaches to St Andrew's and even inviting the national team to base itself in Birmingham before big tournaments. Helping Chinese football is not simply about providing money. '"Probably Chinese football is poorly developed because they have too much money. Mr Yeung has got the money, but he hopes we work together to establish a concept of Chinese football and to make it organised. We will bring in the valuable part of English football."'

Perhaps things sounded too good to be true because on 29 June, Yeung was arrested in Hong Kong on charges of money laundering, relating to a period before his involvement with the club. He was bailed to re-appear in August, his assets were frozen, and the Hong Kong Stock Exchange suspended trading of shares in the club's holding company, Birmingham International Holdings (BIHL), in which Yeung was the single largest shareholder with around 26 per cent.

BIHL appointed acting chairman Peter Pannu and Yeung's 18-year-old son Ryan to the board of the football club, and Michael Wiseman stepped down, ending an 83-year formal association between the club and the Wiseman family. Although it appeared that HSBC, the club's bankers, were unlikely to call in a loan secured on the St Andrew's site. Such a course of action would make it difficult for the club to continue, thus reducing the likelihood of HSBC recovering their money, Yeung's situation impeded the search for new investment.

Such a combination of factors, added to the reduced income to be expected following relegation, left the club in financial difficulty and ready to offload high-earning players, particularly in light of the Football League's adoption of UEFA's financial fair-play regulations relating to clubs not spending in excess of their revenue.

After the shirt sponsorship deal with F&C Investments expired at the end of the 2010/11 season, no long-term sponsor met the value the club set on the brand, so they chose to sell advertising on the shirt on a match-by-match basis. This had the by-product of replica shirts being sold without advertising.

However, a one-year shirt sponsorship deal was reached ironically with a foreign exchange and money transfer company, RationalFX. It emerged that the club had taken legal action against kit manufacturers Xtep for using a derivative version of the club's logo on their own leisurewear, thus infringing intellectual property rights and reducing royalties from sales of officially licensed clothing on the Chinese market. A transfer embargo was placed on the club by the Football League after the club's accounts had not been submitted by the due date.

In May 2016 in Hong Kong the trial of Yeung on five charges of money-laundering between 2001 and 2007 in relation to sums totalling HK$721m (£55m) began. After numerous delays, he was found guilty some nine months later. Trial judge Douglas Yau found him 'not a witness of truth. I find that he is someone who is prepared to and did try to, lie whenever he saw the need to do so!' He was sentenced to six years' imprisonment, and filed notice of appeal. As the season began, progress had been made on satisfying the preconditions for trading in shares of holding company Birmingham International Holdings (BIH) to resume on the Hong Kong Stock Exchange (HKSE). The company took out a loan for reasons of liquidity on 1 August, and weeks later announced attempts to restructure existing debt and the intention of seeking more loan finance for both company and club.

In November, Yeung had agreed to write off a £15m loan to the club in return for shares in BIH. He resigned from all positions within both club and holding company on 4 February, and within days, trading resumed in BIH shares after a two-and-a-half-year suspension. In consequence, the Football League were 'satisfied that Birmingham City complies with its requirements regarding ownership, as well as having funding arrangements in place until at least the end of the season 2013/14', and after BIH vice-chairman Ma Shui Cheong (Yeung's brother-in-law) and investment banker Panos Pavlakis (his future brother-in-law) joined Yeung's son on the football club board, Pannu insisted that Yeung would not be exerting any influence by proxy over the running of the club.

On 11 July 2016, Yeung lost his appeal against a six-year sentence for money laundering. He was jailed in March 2014 having been found guilty of five counts. During his trial, Yeung was unable to show where almost HK$100m (£7.7m) in his bank accounts had come from. He was later freed on bail pending his appeal but Hong Kong's Court of Final Appeal issued a judgement dismissing his case.

A statement from the court said, 'In his Notice of Appeal, Yeung asks that the judgment of the Court of Appeal in CACC 101/2014 dated 13 May 2015 be reversed, varied or altered or that he might have such other relief as this Court should determine.

'No basis has been made out for such relief and his appeal is dismissed.'

The club's new owners – Trillion Trophy Asia – have promised not to sell Blues for at least two years.

Chief executive Peter Pannu's service contract expired at the end of September 2014, though he remained a director, and his *de facto* successor Panos Pavlakis claimed the club was in a sounder financial state than previously.

In December, following comments on the Often Partisan website by someone believed to be Pannu, the club issued a statement that 'categorically refuted' allegations about their tax affairs and funding status, and the Football League asked the club for an explanation. A few days later, Pannu resigned his directorship of the club, and his appointment as CEO and MD of BIH was terminated.

Relationships within BIH became increasingly factional. At the company's AGM in January 2015, Pannu was re-elected to the board while three directors, including Pavlakis, were not, yet the next day the three were reinstated. The Football League made public their concerns over Yeung's attempts to impose his choice of directors on the BIHL board despite his conviction disqualifying him from exerting influence over a club. On 17 February, the board voluntarily appointed receivers from accountants Ernst & Young to take over management of the company. Their statement stressed that no winding-up petition had been issued and the company was not in liquidation, and the receivers assured the League that the club was not in an 'insolvency event' of the type that could trigger a ten-point deduction.

Colin Tattum recalls:

'My experiences with Carson Yeung were mixed. I found him a fascinating, enigmatic figure. When his operation Grandtop International Holdings, the takeover vehicle, owned less than 30 per cent of the shares and Yeung and his entourage came over to Birmingham for a press conference, he was quiet, shy and reticent.

'However, when it acquired all the shares and he became the club's owner outright, the change was marked. He breezed into St Andrew's in the style of an American president, flashing smiles, exuding style, success and a sense of importance. Alas, we now know that the empire was built on sand.'

Michael Dunford recalls:

'I received a telephone call from a football agent in August 2009 asking me if I was interested in talking to Birmingham City. Obviously I was because at that time it was a Premier League club and the Blues were and still are what I call a "proper" football club: traditional, working-class and in the shadows of an "aristocratic" club in the same city i.e. Aston Villa. It was the same for Everton in comparison to Liverpool and therefore I understood the situation. I had two meetings with Peter Pannu in London and an agreement was reached fairly quickly. There was as I remember only one other candidate who was then working for Arsenal so I was delighted to be offered the opportunity of returning to the Premier League.

'On arriving at St Andrew's I was fortunate to inherit from Karren Brady a group of first-class staff members. Julia Shelton who as club secretary is a superb administrator, commercial manager Adrian Wright, sales manager Ian Dutton, HR manager Joanne Allsopp, the list is endless. They were all very focussed and loved the club.

'With any club under new ownership it is vital from day one to establish a close link with all sections of the support. I decided to engage with the local supporters' clubs and held forum sessions on a monthly basis to keep the fans up to date with what was happening at their club. My relationship with the manager Alex McLeish was excellent as I had always made it my business to establish a close working relationship with all the managers I had worked with [like] Joe Royle, Walter Smith, David Moyes, Arthur Cox and Tony Pulis to name but a few.

'They were all extremely professional men but as you would expect had different thoughts on how the game should be played. My belief is that as administrators it's our duty to create an off-the-field team capable of offering the fullest support to the manager and the players. A winning team and a thriving community scheme are the two best marketing tools any CEO can wish for. At St Andrew's we were blessed with both.

'My tenure at St Andrew's was all too short and people will find this hard to understand but I still count my six months at St Andrew's among the happiest I have experienced in over 40 years in football administration. That's apart from the final two days when I think it fair to say my working relationship with Peter Pannu totally disintegrated.

'Peter was Carson Yeung's right-hand man and obviously Peter had that strength behind him. I could go in to details over the reasons for my resignation but suffice it to say Peter took exception to the way I dealt with one particular matter involving Alex and on a matter of principle and staying true to my beliefs I tendered my resignation and left immediately.

'A sad day for me but I would make the same decision again if I was faced with similar circumstances.

'Life is about decisions and consequences and the support I received from the staff and supporters was extremely touching. The Blues will always have a place in my heart.

'Following the Chinese takeover Mike Wiseman and I tried to convince Trevor Francis to become an ambassador for BCFC but despite our best efforts we were unable to convince Trevor to relinquish his attractive position with Sky. That was a blow.'

My wife and son were invited into the boardroom by Mike Wiseman and his family to enable me to present a collection of my books to the new owner of the Blues. It was the Tottenham Hotspur game immediately after the midweek fixture against Aston Villa that had turned into a riot!

The Blues' boardroom is a two-room arrangement; there is an outer area when food is served and visiting directors are entertained and then an inner area which is for specially invited guests only but also houses the toilets. This section is sumptuously decorated but without great class and the toilet is a montage of gold-plated accessories, again expensive but not classy.

There was much activity going on as Richard Scudamore, chief executive of the Premier League ,was there to meet with Carson Yeung and Peter Pannu to discuss the events of the previous Wednesday. Blues had beaten Villa 2-1 in the quarter-final of the Carling Cup with a late winner from Zigic.

Sadly, thousands of Birmingham supporters chose to celebrate our win by charging the length of the field to taunt the Villa fans, generating an angry reaction, with police forced to move in as flares were thrown. It was a disappointing end to what had been a great game, denying us the chance to celebrate with our players.

The kick-off time was 'decided' with television interests to the fore, so the outcome was almost inevitable when fans have so much time to drink prior to the kick-off. It is not an excuse in my mind but it was certainly a contributory factor to the riot occurring.

Not surprisingly the food contained a Chinese option and very good it was. At our table were the Wiseman family with Mike entertaining his sister and mother as well as his good friend Richard Lucas and the Dixons. We were enjoying our pre-match meal when in swept Carson Yeung in a full-length fur coat, which fascinated everyone, especially our ladies. After some discussion as to what fur it might be I excused myself and entered the inner area to use the facilities. On my way back I took it upon myself to introduce myself to Carson and explain about my book gifts and prior to taking my leave I asked him on behalf of the ladies, 'What kind of fur is your coat?' He replied, 'Artificial.' What a let-down. The first of many?

While queuing for food I was flanked by Daniel Levy and another Spurs director who I did not recognise. I made conversation with him and inevitably asked him that tired old question, 'What do you for a living?' He replied, 'I am director of Aimia,' to which I responded, 'I've not heard of them.' He said, 'I am sure you have, we are the Nectar points company!' What an idiot I felt! It was Keith Mills who founded the Nectar loyalty programme and had been a non-executive director with Spurs since 2006.

Carson Yeung was only interested in one thing about Birmingham City Football Club and that was its Premier League status. Carson had two major interests in China, media and clothing, and he hoped to capitalise on the immense interest in the Far East for Premier League football through both business channels. It seems to me that apart from other matters as soon as we were relegated he lost interest in the club and was never seen at St Andrew's thereafter.

Replica shirts for their third season in charge arrived late and were then found to be in Chinese versions of small, medium and large and therefore had to be returned and replacements provided. At the time the only formal English director was Mike Wiseman who was asked to sign off the cost related to full containers being shipped to and from the Far East. I spoke with Mike at that time and explained the vulnerability of his position and advised him to resign as a director which he did on 11 July 2011.

Tom Ross recalls in his book *The game's gone*, 'Interestingly in 2009/10 I hosted the BCFC Academy awards night and sat next to Peter Pannu. He told me that he didn't get on with Alex McLeish and that he was thinking of getting rid of him and replacing him with Sam Allardyce. However Alex McLeish beat him to it and resigned to take over at Aston Villa that summer.

'How much truth was in the Allardyce story I am unsure – it just may have been bravado from Pannu. However, what was true was that Pannu wanted McLeish out of Blues. I suspect because Big Eck was making it known that he was having to get rid of the club's better players and replace them with those not quite so good.'

After the news that Carson Yeung had been arrested on money-laundering charges, Blues were sinking further into the financial mire and it was made public that the club was up for sale.

However, I was contacted by an old pal of mine, Italian businessman Gianni Paladini, who told me that he was in negotiations with Peter Pannu about buying Blues. I spoke to Pannu who denied any contact with Gianni whatsoever. Gianni sent me copies of documents that had been sent to Pannu so I knew he was being economical with the truth.

On one occasion the *Birmingham Mail*'s Colin Tattum and I were invited to see Pannu in the boardroom. On that day Pannu was dismissive about Yeung and his influence on the football club as it was obvious that Yeung was going to prison. I suspect Pannu thought he would end up being the main man with Yeung out of the way.

He was disgusted about Paladini when I asked if he would ever sell to his consortium. He used the analogy where he likened Paladini to an old female toilet cleaner, saying, 'If you went out to pick up a chick and you were unlucky you might end up going back to the toilet cleaner.'

15

Project Jack

THIS CHAPTER relates the ongoing efforts I am making to secure some sort of ownership of Birmingham City Football Club. Whether I will be successful is very much in doubt, but who knows?

Initially let me explain why I used the expression 'Project Jack' for this adventure. It is in respect of one of the kindest and friendliest men I have met during my time as a Blues supporter and that man is Jack Wiseman. I first met him in 1992 when I was a corporate member of the Captain's Club located in the old stand and immediately understood why he was called 'Jolly' as he had time and a smile for everyone, young and old, and it didn't matter what your status was because to Jack it made no difference. So when my team were looking for a name for our project I suggested Jack and it was adopted immediately not just as a title but also because his name and reputation reflected our key approach to the project – the good of BCFC. Because the project is potentially still active I am unable to identify by name the members of the Project Jack group but the complexion of any such consortium requires the following:

a. The Money Man – someone experienced in financing football club deals

b. The Legal Man – someone who understood football and would ensure that we acted legally
c. The Credibility Man – someone who 'knew' the target club and would give any approach a seal of approval to its status
d. The Front Man – someone who could co-ordinate the process and also 'sell' the idea to all related parties – that's me!

Project Jack was conceived on 27 February 2014 when I was in idle conversation with my friend Simon McLaven, a Chelsea fan, about football and the troubles at Blues, due to the problems with our Chinese owner. Simon knew of my earlier interest in buying the Blues 11 years earlier and casually mentioned that a neighbour of his met the definition of The Money Man and if I was interested he felt sure he could broker a meeting on my behalf.

I have to admit that I was lukewarm to the idea but then by coincidence in early March I heard Michael Dunford on the radio talking about the ownership situation at St Andrew's and as I had met and befriended Michael during his short stay as chief executive officer, it just seemed too much of a coincidence to ignore.

I e-mailed Michael on 6 March outlining my idea which had been spawned by the following news item:

'Up to five groups were reportedly interested in buying the club, but BIH were willing only to dispose of tranches, as sale of the whole club would leave the company with no business and hence they would lose their HKSE listing again. Trading in shares in the club's parent company, Birmingham International Holdings (BIH), was suspended in June 2011 after the arrest of major shareholder Carson Yeung on charges of money-laundering. Publication of financial results was repeatedly delayed, which led the Football League to impose a transfer embargo, and offers for the club were entertained from 2012 onwards. After Yeung resigned his positions with both club and BIH in early 2014, share trading resumed and following his conviction, efforts intensified to dispose of the club, which had to be done piecemeal in order to retain BIH's share listing.'

The issue was that to retain its share listing BIH had to have within its structure a trading company. Apparently there is no place on the Hong Kong Stock Exchange for 'shell companies' so I decided to create a situation which enabled new owners to take over the football side of Blues and leave BIH with a venue business. This would mean it would retain its share listing while enabling it to acquire another trading company which would enable it to sell the venue business to the owners of the footballing business.

It was obvious that retention of BIH's Hong Kong stock market listing was key to any offer and my e-mail to Michael included the following:

'The general idea is to buy Wast Hills, the playing staff and all costs related to what happens on the pitch with a long-term lease to use St Andrew's on matchdays, thereby leaving Pannu et al to run the venue!

'The financial model would be matchday receipts, player and team sponsorship together with TV money etc. to Newco with merchandise, corporate hospitality and everything else to the venue.

'Whether or not this stacks up financially, the question to you is: Would the FA and League allow such a structure to operate?'

Michael replied the following day, saying, 'Many thanks for your e-mail – sounds like an interesting project you are embarking on. I wish you every success as the club requires a stable management structure to try and re-build its reputation and provide the financial certainty to grow the business. If you think it helpful I don't mind meeting up with you in the near future to discuss your ideas.' After an exchange of e-mails we agreed to meet at the Village Hotel in Walsall on Tuesday 1 April.

The project was gaining its own momentum and it was time to take some legal advice so I spoke to The Legal Man, who confirmed, 'The FA has no issue with separation of Stadium and "Club" provided that the club has a right to occupy the stadium and the club has the right to play football at the stadium. In addition the buyer of the club must have a "proprietary interest" in playing football.'

My meeting with The Money Man was held on 21 March 2014 at The Randolph Hotel in Oxford. We had an interesting two-and-a-half-hour chat during which he informed me of his top-level connections throughout football and some of his recent successful transactions.

I explained my idea regarding the Blues and he promised to go away and think about it. He responded to me the following evening, saying, 'This looks a very fluid situation and certainly qualifies for "up in the air" status. My interpretation of your points is that if this develops into something concrete, my position would be representing the buyer rather than the owner of the club, which is the alternative route.'

This was agreed and I decided to find out more background information through my business contacts. They understood that there had been two independent valuations of the club which were between £8m and £10m. It was inevitable that the club would run out of cash and therefore a possibility in the future could have been to buy off any appointed administrator but that was a remote option as Blues were due a parachute payment of £6m at the end of the season. There was also a rumour that the Chinese were demanding substantial cash payments for meetings with interested purchasers. I made the decision immediately that such a payment was never going to happen with my group.

With every deal, in its embryonic stages there are times when you have to reconsider the validity of the proposition. This was one such moment and I felt it was definitely worth moving the matter forward, so I signed a terms of engagement letter with The Legal Man's law firm and we had made progress.

The information coming out of the club at the time was that a price tag of £32m was being quoted on a frequent basis and that only 25 per cent of the club was for sale at a price of £8m. There was no clear future plan as to when the remaining 75 per cent would be for sale or if the minority shareholder would have any say in the day-to-day management of BCFC. The familiar concern about the Hong Kong Stock Exchange was clearly paramount for BIHL and it had to purchase another business before it relinquished control of the club.

Another reality check was required. I could not believe that anyone in their right mind would contemplate going down this route as I felt that a maximum value for the club (i.e. for 96.5 per cent BIHL stake and BIHL inter-company loan of approximately £18m) was £10m at best and probably getting nearer to £6m as time progressed. I could also foresee a situation where if anyone was daft enough to pay £8m for the 25 per cent stake then they could be approached by the Chinese to put more money into the club as a loan to keep the business afloat as well as having no control on how the money was spent.

What did The Money Man think? He responded that the prevailing wisdom is that £10m is the price ceiling and the moment of maximum opportunity appears to be when the cash erosion forces the owners to rethink their stance about the asking price and the acquisition mechanic. Of course, the trick was going to lie in judging when that moment was. He was still looking at candidate buyers and naturally he wanted to be armed with a mandate prior to engagement with Carson/AN Other, in what he hoped would end up as a rapid transaction. At this stage in mid-April the project was still on.

The amount of press activity was increasing around this time with speculation rife about so many aspects surrounding the club that it was important that we declared a formal interest in buying the Blues.

On 9 May the group spent most of the day at the Blue Bird Café on the King's Road in Chelsea to discuss our approach in detail. The following questions were posed and answered:

- Do we have the finance to make a bid? Yes – two potentials
- What level of offer should it be? £10m plus transfer kitty
- How and who will make the approach? – The Legal Man direct to the company secretary of BIHL

Our interest was declared to BIHL by e-mail with a copy to Panos Pavlakis of BCFC on 12 May 2014 at 4.44pm. By 5.27pm Panos replied to The Legal Man as follows, 'My name is Panos Pavlakis and I am an executive director in both BIHL and BCFC.

'I am flying back to Hong Kong tonight as we are currently working on many fronts (including a possible disposal). Any potential expression of interest could be sent to me directly as I am working on this subject for some time now here in the UK.'

On 30 May the *Birmingham Mail* reported that Soccer Management Worldwide Limited, with Jeremy Wray (ex-Swindon Town) as The Front Man, had been granted a three-week exclusivity period to complete final due diligence in order to fully assess the opportunity.

On 10 June Sky Sports News reported that Adam Pearson, at the time owner of Hull FC, had entered the race to buy BCFC.

On 13 June I formed the company Birmingham Football Limited to act as the vehicle for our offer.

On 27 June I was informed that BIHL had promised to inject £7m into the club to keep it alive and had made representations to the Football League that it would do this and had already lodged £3m.

Frustrated by the lack of progress, I decided to set up a meeting with Panos which took place on 30 July 2014 at St Andrew's. I was accompanied by The Legal Man. The content of that meeting is under a mutual confidential agreement but suffice it to say that he liked our concept and agreed to take it forward to BIHL in late August/early September.

After a further meeting in London I experienced another reality check. Why would an investor be interested in buying the Blues? I came up with the following:

1. A business/club that bears the name of a major UK city

2. Recent success at national level – 2010/2011 – Carling Cup winners

3. Recent experience of the Premier League

4. A stadium and associated property to Premier League standard

5. Asset value of business

6. Potential attendance of 30k+ for 25+ matches per season

7. International prestige gained

8. Stadium has development opportunity to increase capacity by 6,000 minimum

9. Team presenting opportunity has a breadth of skills/

experience to add value both in short and medium term to investment

10. No Crown or bank debts – working capital requirement of £7.5m

So in my mind it still made sense. However, nothing transpired as promised during the autumn of 2014, and the whole proposition went into stalled mode.

Not wishing to leave things as they were, I e-mailed Andre Wong and Billy Tang, who were working with Ernst Young, the receivers appointed by BIHL on 17 April 2015, 'We would like to enter any process you establish, should yourselves and Ernst Young decide that it is in the interest of BIHL to divest itself of the football club. In short our proposal at the time of talking to Panos was based on a deal that would enable BIHL to retain its HKSE listing.

'My team would initially purchase the footballing entity of BCFC from BIHL. This would leave BIHL with an arena business i.e. St Andrew's and some money – thereby enabling it to retain its HKSE listing while having the funds to buy another business. Alongside our purchase of the footballing entity, we would enter into an agreement with BIHL to rent the arena for the fulfilment of the football commitments of BCFC together with an agreement to purchase the arena over a three-year period.'

The following day I received this reply, 'Dear Keith, Thank you very much for your interest in acquiring BCFC. We are sorry to inform you that the deadline for submitting an indicative offer has already passed and the result shall be released shortly. To be fair to other bidders, I am afraid we will not be able to consider your offer at this time. Thank you very much for your understanding. Regards Andre.'

In October 2016 Birmingham City finally ended its seven-year association with Carson Yeung when Chinese firm Trillion Trophy Asia (TTA) acquired more than 50 per cent of shares in the club. The deal was delayed until Birmingham International Holdings resumed trading on the Hong Kong Stock Exchange after protracted negotiations with ex-employees, shareholders and the appointed receivers, Ernst Young, who had been running the club since 2015 after BIHL went into receivership.

Trillion Trophy Asia Limited and BCFC plc is constituted in the British Virgin Islands (BVI) but its trading address is Room 1501, 15th Floor, Great Eagle Centre, 23 Harbour Road, Wanchai, Hong Kong.

Peter Suen, who controls TTA, was granted a two-year exclusivity period to negotiate the purchase of Blues.

In the Poly Investments Holdings Limited Annual Report 2006 in the section entitled 'Biographical details of Directors and Senior Management', Paul Suen's details are:

'Mr Suen Cho Hung, Paul, aged 46, has been Chairman of the Company since July 2002. Mr Suen holds a Master of Business Administration degree from the University of South Australia. Prior to joining the Company, he was chief executive of several private enterprises and has over 15 years of experience in international trading of metals, minerals and raw materials, manufacturing of metal products, property investment as well as management and corporate planning of industrial enterprises in the People's Republic of China (the 'PRC'). Mr Suen is a substantial shareholder of the Company, as disclosed in the section headed "Interests of Shareholders Discloseable under the SFO" in the Directors' Report.'

Panos Pavlakis, who has been in charge of the day-to-day running of operations as a director since 2014, has an unclear future even though he has performed well in keeping the club in existence but his personal relationship with Carson Yeung may well define his future. The manner in which the board will function under Suen's ownership is also unclear.

With four West Midlands clubs now under Chinese ownership, after Dr Tony Xia's takeover of Aston Villa, the sale of West Bromwich Albion to a Chinese investment group and Chinese conglomerate Fosun International's purchase of Wolverhampton Wanderers, I believe there is a general antipathy to the Chinese which will be counter-productive to Suen's plans.

It is obvious that TTA is not cash-rich but it has been putting money in over recent times which indicates its intentions to support as best it can the development of the club and its infrastructure. Its statement that it will not sell the club for two years is a little bizarre in these circumstances but at least signposts a period of stability behind the scenes.

This prompted my e-mail to Andre Wong and Billy Tang of Goldin Financial Limited in Hong Kong, who had received my notification of interest in purchasing the club. The e-mail was sent at 5.29pm on 13 June 2016:

> Good Evening Andre and Billy
> I e-mailed you in April 2015 regarding my plans to acquire Birmingham City Football Club, you very kindly replied stating 'that the deadline for submitting an indicative offer has already passed....I am afraid we will not be able to consider your offer at this time.'
>
> As you would appreciate I have kept a close watch on the situation and was pleased to see the statement from Panos outlining the plans being progressed by the prospective new owners, Trillion Trophy Asia.
>
> The purpose of my e-mail is to make an offer to you, as the advisors to Mr Suen Cho Hung Paul, to help with the integration of the takeover assuming it goes ahead.

Within the City of Birmingham and not just with the supporters of Birmingham City Football Club there is a level of negativity and apathy to the thought of another Chinese owner taking over the club after the experiences with Carson Yeung (particularly with the new potential owner of Aston Villa being of Chinese descent).

I believe that Mr Suen Cho Hung Paul and Trillion Trophy Asia need to have initial support from Birmingham business people in establishing a corporate governance approach to the running of the club on a day-to-day basis as well as planning for the future development of the football club. I believe it would also be advantageous to the new owners if those business people were long-standing Birmingham City supporters.

I am aware that Mr Suen Cho Hung Paul believes in corporate governance as when he was Chairman of Poly Investments Holdings Limited he had an Independent Non-Executive Director appointed to the Board in the form of Mr Sun Ka Ziang Henry.

As a current Independent Non-Executive Director/Chairman with a number of companies in the UK (as well as being a supporter of the Blues for 61 years) I am offering my services as an Independent Non-Executive Director to act free-of-charge for an initial three month period to help the integration of the takeover.

Within these initial three months I will establish a Board of Directors to include Mr Suen Cho Hung Paul (as Chairman) and his delegated Executive Directors plus appointing other Directors who have a love of the club and specific skills e.g. Football

Association registered lawyer, establish a monthly
Board Meeting regime working to a formal agenda
and I will also provide a communication conduit
between the club and the fan base.

I look forward to hearing your response to this
offer.

Regards
Keith Dixon

The reply was not long coming, arriving at 3.09am on 14
June:

Dear Mr. Dixon,
Thanks for your email. However, we are not in the
position to appoint any directors or any personnel.
I have copied your email to the Receivers in this
email for their consideration.

Best Regards,
Billy

The e-mail was sent to Gilbert Ho and David Yen of Ernst
Young.

By 8 November I was still waiting for a reply. Then the
news broke that day that three new Chinese directors
from Birmingham International Holdings (BIH) had been
appointed to the plc board: Wenqing Zhao, born in October
1966, to act as chairman and receive an annual salary of
£180,000; Chun Kong Yiu, born in November 1984, as a
director and receiving an annual salary of £24,000; and Zhu
Kai, born in September 1986, receiving the same salary as
Chun Kong Yiu. Three new directors, aged 50, 32 and 30,
with no experience of English corporate law and taking out
of the club a total of £224,000 in salaries.

Just over a month later, on Wednesday 14 December, the club terminated the contract of manager Gary Rowett with immediate effect along with Kevin Summerfield, Mark Sale and Kevin Poole. This was the first outward sign of how the new board would operate. It was commercially motivated, clinically administered and evidence of the club wishing to take a new direction. There is nothing particularly wrong with that but obviously the surprise announcement was accentuated by the fact that Gary and his team were ex-Blues players and they had done a great job in rescuing the club from the prospect of League 1 and creating a squad of players that was competing in the Championship.

Clearly the new board had been working behind the scenes and by the same evening it was announced that Gianfranco Zola was taking over the manager's role on a two-and-a-half-year contract, with his team of Pierluigi Casiraghi and Gabriele Cioffic as first team coaches, Kevin Hitchcock as goalkeeper coach and Sebastiano Porcu as video analyst. It was clear that the name of 50-year-old Zola would be more effective than Rowett in establishing the brand of Birmingham City in China.

He was a great footballer, with a career including 35 appearances and ten goals for Italy, but his management credentials are limited; two years at West Ham United, one year looking after the Italian under-18s, less than two years at Watford, and two short spells with Cagliari and Al-Arabi.

On that evening I sent this e-mail to Panos Pavlakis:

Evening Panos
I know this must be a difficult time for you but rest assured if I can help in any way just let me know.
    The antipathy towards Chinese ownership will be even more intense following the dismissal of the Rowett management team so if you would like

an English Bluenose to act as a Non-Executive
Director I would be happy to take on that role for
three months at no cost to the club.

I do not come with a £24,000 per annum fee,
my average rate for my 9 Non-Executive Chairman
roles is £700/month or £8,400 per annum!

Regards
Keith

Although I received an immediate 'read receipt' reply I have
yet to receive a reply and I did not expect one.

At 3.37pm on Tuesday 20 December I received the
following e-mail reply from Panos:

Hi Keith,
Thank you for your email, that was a Board
Decision and I think we got it cover now.

Regards,
Panos

I am not sure what it means but I guess they do not want to
take me up on my offer.

Just as a benchmark the Companycheck website gives the
following information on Birmingham City FC plc:

Cash: £2.5m

Net Worth: (£5.625m) – yes, that's a negative figure

Assets: £9.1m

Liabilities: £24.9m

Let's see how the business performs to the end of the
current season and where the team finishes in the Championship.

16

Did You Know That?

ON 30 OCTOBER 2016 Roy Smiljanic celebrated his 1,000th first team game as the club's official photographer.

Roy is a massive fan of the Blues and in 2006 he possessed an incredible collection of club memorabilia, the prized item of which was the boots worn by Darren Carter when he scored the penalty that took Birmingham into the Premier League for the first time in their history.

* * * *

Colin Buchanan, who played Pascoe in the television detective series *Dalziel and Pascoe*, is a season ticket holder. Colin is currently working for the impresario Bill Kenwright in period dramas in theatres around the country. This schedule means that he has to miss a number of home matches so he asked Bill if he would reimburse him the cost of his season ticket. Kenwright refused, thinking Colin was not serious, but he was – even the chairman of Everton does not understand the mentality of a Bluenose. Colin is a celebrity fan who actually attends his club's matches unlike David Cameron, Prince William and Tom Hanks who perhaps just like to be associated with a team with a quirky name?

* * * *

Kenny Cunningham, during his heyday, used to travel to home games in a Ford Mondeo with a W registration plate!

* * * *

Winston Foster was Gil Merrick's gardener.

* * * *

When Gil Merrick's Rover became too big for him to handle as a pensioner, Phil Hawker, who owns a second-hand car business in Bromsgrove and scored one goal in 37 appearances for the Blues between 1978 and 1983, sorted him out with a modest Volvo.

* * * *

On 15 May 2008 I wrote to Noel Kinsey in Norwich asking him for his memories on Gil Merrick as a contribution to my biography on the great man. I received a reply, which was my letter returned with a hand-written message saying, 'I have no interest in football past or present.'

* * * *

Ian Atkins went to the same school as me, Sheldon Heath Comprehensive, and one of his teachers was Brian Clements who played in the same pop group as me in the early 1960s – The Amazons.

* * * *

The 1992/93 Triton Showers-sponsored shirt, which was so maligned at the time, is for sale on the website www. classicfootballshirts.co.uk with a medium-sized shirt costing £89.99.

* * * *

In July 1991 I submitted a game show format to Granada Television called *Go For Goal*. On 25 July I received a rejection letter from Dianne Nelmes, executive producer: entertainment, stating, 'I really have no chance of developing anything like this at present.'

The idea was to have two teams representing a football club, made up of a celebrity fan and a player from that club. Imagine my surprise when in a 1996 Blues publication Gary Ablett related the tale that he had been involved in a pilot for a game show which comprised of two teams, one representing Everton which included Gary (player) and John Parrott (celebrity fan) and the other representing Liverpool with Duncan McKenzie (celebrity fan) and David Johnston (player). The host was Elton Welsby and the season of the pilot was 1991/92. The production company was Granada Television.

This was too much of a coincidence so I wrote to Bill Hilary, editor of light entertainment at Granada Television, outlining the situation and asking for a copy of the pilot for which I provided a self-addressed envelope and offered to reimburse any costs. That was on 28 November 1996 and on 5 December I received a reply from Adam Oliver, business affairs manager, who had copied in Bill Hilary and a Kieran Roberts, stating, 'I have spoken to the producer of this show who has confirmed that he developed the format and name himself along with a research team, that it was not based upon any submission that you or any other external person made to Granada, and that he was never aware of your proposal. In the circumstances we consider it inappropriate to supply you with a copy of the programme, but would like to reassure you that we do not consider that your rights have been infringed in any way.' So that's all right then?

* * * *

When Gil Merrick died I was contacted by Jim Holden, a London-based sports journalist, as he was writing an obituary. I was more than happy to help Jim and his work was ultimately published in *The Telegraph* on 5 October 2010.

* * * *

Former Blues forward Ken Leek's grandson is Karl Darlow, the Newcastle United goalkeeper.

* * * *

Jimmy Harris still lives in the terraced house he was born in on 18 August 1933.

* * * *

Martin O'Connor is a qualified freight train driver.

* * * *

Bert Murray, a Blue in the late 1960s, had been Chelsea's first-ever substitute. Brian Sharples holds the same accolade for Birmingham City.

* * * *

Tony Want's daughter Lorna (Want) is playing the part of Cynthia Weil in the show *Beautiful – the Carole King Musical* at the Aldwych Theatre in London.

* * * *

Paul Devlin used to room with Robbie Savage. It was their routine that Robbie went to their room first and hid himself. When Paul got to the room Robbie would jump out and they would fight like Kato and Inspector Clouseau in the Pink Panther movies.

* * * *

When my pal Ken Shaw moved on to the Four Oaks private estate he received a visit from his near neighbour, Doug Ellis, who proceeded to question him on all aspects of his life. After a lengthy discussion Doug got up to leave, and Ken, who is a Villa fan, cheekily asked, 'Sorry Doug, what do you do?' Apparently the look on Doug's face was priceless.

For those readers who do not know what Doug does then let me help. He was a director of Birmingham City Football Club and through his business Ellerman Travel pioneered low-cost flights to European resorts. What he has done since then I haven't a clue.

* * * *

On occasions I can become a grumpy old man and when the Villa were finally relegated from the Premier League after four previous lucky escapes I thought the *Birmingham Mail* might become more even-handed in its coverage of the two clubs. That did not happen so I sent this e-mail:

Dear Sirs

I am sorry to say that at the age of 69 I have decided to no longer purchase the *Birmingham Mail* due to your biased football coverage.

When they were in the Premier League I reconciled your disproportionate coverage of Aston Villa against Birmingham City due to them being part of the top tier in football but today's edition is the straw that broke my back!

The back page is devoted to the Villa along with pages 54 and 55 while Blues are on page 51 which is shared with Wolverhampton Wanderers.

Both clubs are in the second tier now and hopefully in the future, although I will not see it, your coverage will be more even-handed, although I doubt it.

Why do I doubt it? Because it is inbred into your newspaper's culture i.e. most references to the Villa manager are 'Robbie' while Gary is referred to as 'Rowett' – just one example.

Little things mean a lot to your readers.

Not surprisingly I received no response but I have not bought a *Mail* or *Mercury* since.

* * * *

Jimmy Harris was told by his then manager Gil Merrick that if he had got married he would have been an England regular!

* * * *

England international Fred Pickering was barred from the International Lounge at Ewood Park because he did not get his representative honours while playing for Blackburn Rovers. He approached the lounge with fellow Rovers internationals Ronnie Clayton and Bryan Douglas, who would have been allowed in. To their credit they refused to go in if Fred was barred.

* * * *

Howard Kendall could not believe the fanaticism of the Bluenoses. At the end of the 1973/74 season Blues beat Norwich City 2-1 to stave off relegation. Howard was captain at the time and was enjoying a post-match soak when Freddie Goodwin came in and told him to get the players out on the pitch for a lap of honour as the fans would not leave the stadium. Howard had never before performed a lap of honour for avoiding relegation!

* * * *

For 2016/17 the corporate hospitality package in the Jasper Carrott Suite includes:

- Champagne reception upon arrival
- Full 45-minute behind-the-scenes stadium tour
- Luxury four-course meal
- Exclusive panoramic pitch views while you dine
- Half-time refreshments
- Complimentary bar throughout the day (beers, wines and soft drinks)
- Man-of-the-match interview and presentation
- Dedicated host/hostess for the day
- BCFC Star of the Day interview
- Matchday programme for each guest
- Three car parking spaces on the Kop car park

All for the princely sum of £99 + VAT per person

* * * *

Karren Brady featured in *Private Eye* issue 1,416 on 15 April 2016: 'Teenagers and porn is the subject of a column by Karren Brady in *The Sun*. "You don't want them thinking it is normal for boys to treat girls as objects," she writes. "Let's face it, very few pornos show a loving couple enjoying healthy sex."

'No doubt this is a point she has made very forcefully over the years to her employers, West Ham co-owners David Gold and David Sullivan, who made much of their fortune in porn magazines and blue movies.'

* * * *

As you walk along the tunnel under the Gil Merrick Stand from the Kop you pass on the left-hand side the following doors: mascots' room, away dressing room, officials' room, matchday flash interview room, treatment room, doping control station, kitchen, home dressing room and manager's office and then you are out of the tunnel on to the pitch.

* * * *

Most football clubs have press rooms where the managers will hold post-match press conferences. But first the managers will visit the flash interview room, where a single television camera provides a feed to broadcasters who have bought the rights to live coverage or recorded highlights of the game.

* * * *

After you have entered the Kop Stand via reception you climb up the stairs to the first floor where you will see immediately in front of you a display of framed shirts from 1992 to today. To the left is the corridor to the Legends Lounge and if you turn right you go into the Boardroom Lounge which leads to the boardroom.

On the landing at the top of the stairs are four display cabinets. To the left of the stairs is a small cabinet entitled 'From the Archives' which contains a letter from Small Heath Football Club dated 25 September 1902, a photograph of the Blues team of 1948, a letter from manager Bob McRoberts dated 27 March 1913, a letter from manager George Liddell dated 12 February 1935, and a copy of the Harry Hibbs souvenir programme dated 13 April 1940. To the right of the stairs is a three-part display which features memorabilia under three headings: Heritage, Finals and Europe.

17

Stadium Project

ON 2 JUNE 2016 I received the following e-mail:

'Hi Keith. I hope this e-mail finds you well. Let me introduce myself, my name is Rosie Lesurf and I am a producer at The Birmingham Repertory Theatre. At The Rep we are about to embark on a new project that is all about the wonderful devoted football fans of Birmingham. The project is being led by internationally successful director, Mohamed El Khatib and will have high profile in the theatre and with local football organisations. The project is entitled Stadium.

'We are looking to conduct a series of informal interviews with football fans and figureheads, listening to their stories and learning about their passions and relationships with their team. Mohamed would really like to meet with you, pick your brains on your extensive local football knowledge and is especially interested in your publications, including the book about the rivalry between Birmingham City and Villa.

'Interviews will be very friendly and informal and can happen at a time and day to suit you. The

232

project will have a high profile and will culminate in a performance on The Rep's main stage in June 2017, reaching large numbers of audiences and fans. It would be great to hear back from you as to whether you'd be happy to support the project and I know Mohamed is really keen to meet you.

'My number is at the bottom of this email if you'd prefer to talk about this over the phone or alternatively I can call you to discuss it further. I very much look forward to hearing from you. Best Wishes Rosalyn Lesurf-Olner Community Engagement Producer.'

I exchanged e-mails with Rosie and understood that Stadium was part of a three-year community programme entitled Furnace. It was agreed that I would meet Rosie and Mohamed at the Marmalade bar at The Rep at midday on Monday 6 June.

Well it was some 'informal interview'. I was interviewed direct to camera with no prior knowledge of the questions to be asked. As well as Mohamed and Rosie, there was a cameraman and an interpreter.

They spent an hour and 15 minutes interviewing me about the Blues and our relationship with the Villa, together with my memories of being a supporter for so long. The interview culminated in my singing 'Keep Right On' without musical accompaniment.

On 10 August I received this e-mail:

'Thank you very much for getting involved in Stadium with Birmingham Repertory Theatre and Mohamed El Khatib back in June this year. Mohamed thoroughly enjoyed meeting you and hearing your stories and passion come alive for

your team. We created a short promotional video
as a result of his first visit which is now available
on our website and will help us get more amazing
fans involved!'

The link was only on the website for a short time but it
featured a number of Blues fans, including Lynda and Peter
Courts who organise the Redditch Supporters' Club. Also
interviewed were Carol 'Scarf Lady' Butcher and Lee Neal,
who helped set up the Tilton Alliance, plus others.

The production is scheduled to play from 9 to 17 June
2017 and is described as, 'One crowd sharing one colour, one
song and one wish. Every goal and every near miss brings a
pride almost too much to bear. Winning is amazing.

'Following the success of our co-production with the
National Theatre of Jeremy Deller's award-winning *We're
Here Because We're Here*, The REP has commissioned
acclaimed French director Mohamed El Khatib for the
second show in our Furnace series.

'In this pioneering world premiere, hundreds of Aston
Villa, Birmingham City, and West Bromwich Albion fans
unite to share their surprising, funny, heart-breaking stories.
From friendships formed to partners left behind, all aspects
of fandom are explored.

'Inspired by his father's love of the sport, acclaimed
theatre maker Mohamed El Khatib explores why football
inspires passion like nothing else. Just why is "the beautiful
game" so beautiful?'

STADIUM PROJECT

The creative team was listed as:

Director and Creator	Mohamed El Khatib
Designer	Fred Hocke
Associate Director	Keziah Surreau
Choreographer and Performer	Dimitri Hatton
Assistant Director	Gavin Thatcher

On 20 December 2016 I received the following update from Rosalyn:

> 'Hi Keith
> Mohamed is still busy meeting with different fans. He was overwhelmed by the number of lovely Blues fans he met and is now concentrating on just meeting Villa fans to even things out a bit! In the New Year he will be looking to condense his thinking and ideas down for the creation of the show. I'll keep you posted!'

18

Behind the Numbers

AT THE time of writing (November 2016), Birmingham City Football Club plc was listed on the website Companycheck to have £4.6m in cash, a net worth of £1.5m, assets of £8.5m and liabilities of £17m.

It is the responsibility of the directors of any company to ensure that the business is operated legally demonstrating financial probity and with the objective of growing shareholder value. A board of directors should also operate with the well-being of all stakeholders i.e. shareholders, customers, employees, suppliers etc. at the forefront of its operations.

The directors of Birmingham City Football Club since 1992 were:

Name	Date of Appointment	Date of Termination
Jack Francis Wiseman	31/12/1990	14/08/2009
Samesh Kumar	31/12/1990	25/01/1993
Ramesh Kumar	31/12/1990	25/01/1993
Bimal Kumar	31/12/1990	25/01/1993
Terence Cooper	17/10/1991	29/11/1993
Bryan Hilton Slater	23/12/1991	16/08/1993
Alan Graham Jones	17/12/1992	24/09/2002

David Sullivan	06/03/1993	06/10/2009
Baroness Karren Rita Brady	06/03/1993	06/09/2009
Bradley Gold	25/09/1993	19/12/2007
David Gold	16/10/1993	09/11/2009
Ralph Gold	16/10/1993	12/10/2009
Henri Brandman	12/01/1994	13/10/2009
Michael John Wiseman	13/12/1997	11/07/2011
Perry Brian Deakin	01/07/2005	31/05/2007
Ka Sing Carson Yeung	13/10/2009	04/02/2014
Vico Ho Leuk Hui	13/10/2009	10/07/2012
Ryan Tsz Tsung Yeung	11/07/2011	11/08/2015
Peter Pannu	11/07/2011	12/12/2014
Panogiotis Pavlakis	01/01/2014	
Shui Cheong Ma	01/01/2014	
Wenqing Zhao	08/11/2016	
Chun Kong Yiu	08/11/2016	
Zhu Kai	08/11/2016	

The numbers are:

Company Performance

Year Ending 31/08	Profit Before Taxation	Shareholders' Funds/(Deficit)	Turnover	Directors' Drawings	Players
1993	(£798,472)	(£1,960,277)	£3,120,644	£85,167	50
1994	(£1,131,157)	(£3,090,784)	£3,763,132	£86,080	60
1995	£256,083	(£2,833,901)	£6,941,671	£79,502	53
1996	(£1,866.588)	(£4,701,239)	£7,337,071	£101,133	41
1997	£1,124,773	(£3,631,677)	£7,622,186	£125,163	49
1998	(£3,668,112)	(£7,244,578)	£8,336,859	£127,034	37
1999	£2,890,306	(£2,890,306)	£8,431,225	£143,474	41

2000	£1,531,552	(£1,531,552)	£9,403,965	£170,918	46
2001	(£2,625,951	(£7,242,240)	£13,286,713	£248,933	52
2002	(£6,400,715)	(£13,588,860)	£15,184,036	£242,773	57
2003	£3,341,334	(£10,250,876)	£36,480,196	£212,926	60
2004	£5,639,896	(£4,476,817)	£45,336,818	£160,353	53
2005	£8,597,514	(£2,912,733)	£42,705,935	£510,119	56
2006	£5,725,986	(£1,161,588)	£40,116,886	£577,972	59
2007	(£6,229,855)	(£2,126,013)	£25,038,980	£1,383,742	47
2008	£4,554,078	£4,554,078	£49,835,665	£896,439	48
Year Ending 30/06					
2009	£1,685,427	(£21,830,775)	£27,509,219	£1,046,137	51
2010	£288,686	(£6,900,654)	£56,422,666	£1,306,807	53
2011	(£11,882,839)	(£19,242,744)	£61,452,609	£80,247	55
2012	£16,405,580	(£3,530,184)	£39,085,870	£687,611	51
2013	(£3,014,529)	(£7,575,844)	£24,198,019	£389,620	51
2014	(£4,622,673)	£535,045	£20,085,748	£223,721	50
2015	£1,342,936	£1,873,524	£21,049,000	Nil	57

At the end of each financial year the board of directors issues the relevant numbers in the Annual Report, which also includes a narrative report from the directors. Here are some snippets from the reports of the last 25 years:

1994
Redevelopment of the Tilton Road and Spion Kop is now almost complete and a planning application is being put forward to rebuild the rest of the ground.

1995
Sport Newspapers has continued to provide support and had invested nearly £6m at 31/08/1995.

1996

Sport Newspapers has increased its financial support by injecting a further £700k during the year. Its debt with the club at 31/08/96 was over £6.5m.

Taken steps to issue shares on the AIM (Alternative Investment Market) in February 1997.

1997

As part of our continuing programme to develop the club, this season we have seen the opening of the new St Andrew's Museum, International Suite and Corner Flag bar. We have also successfully launched a customer care initiative, helping us to improve relationships with our supporters.

1998

During the current year we have seen the launch of our internet site and *Out of the Blue*, our fortnightly newspaper with a readership of 20,000. We have introduced a new Banqueting and Hospitality department which, I am delighted to report, has produced additional profits for the Club. In addition, we have re-launched our membership and lottery department which has resulted in better financial returns.

The completion of the Railway Stand in February 1999 will bring additional commercial opportunities including 16 new executive boxes and executive seating and lounge facilities. The increase in capacity will help us develop greater inroads into encouraging more members of the Birmingham community to become Club supporters.

The opening of the new stand will see the introduction of our new Olympic Gallery area which provides lounge, bar and seating facilities for new season ticket holders. We will have a total of 66 boxes when the new 16 are opened at the start of the 1999/2000 season.

We are delighted to announce that Paul McCartney has chosen our club to launch Linda McCartney's food range in February 1999.

Net spend on new players £5.2m.

1999

Under the new accounting standard FRS10, the Club is now required to capitalise the cost of player registrations and write them off over the life of the relevant contract. Before such amortisation charges and net transfer fees, the operating loss for the year was £211,861 (1998 – profit of £1.168 million). After such costs and interest, the result for the year was an operating loss of £2.89 million (1998 – loss of £1.68 million).

As a result of the Bosman ruling, the Board has also been under pressure to offer improved terms to players reaching the end of their original contracts. Overall wage costs have increased to £6.23 million (year ended 31 August 1998 – £5.07 million).

2000

We are currently in the process of negotiating a number of new commercial contracts and to this end the commercial operation of the Club remains one of its strongest attributes. The Club can now boast an offering of a number of non-football-related services to its supporters, including Blues Financial Services offering mortgages, insurance, savings accounts, ISAs, etc. We also have a Blues credit card, Blues petrol card, Blues Telecom, Blues Health Insurance, Blues Funeral Services, Blues Travel and are moving into Blues Gas, Electricity and Water in the new year.

2001

Promotion remains our number one priority and we believe that the appointment of our new manager and his backroom staff will finally bring us the success we have long been striving for. We understand that we will need to increase expenditure to achieve our goal of playing in the Premier League and that the main area affected will be players' wages. Additionally compensation payments made to the previous management team and to Crystal Palace to secure Steve Bruce's release will have an adverse effect on our trading position going forward. We are also committed to building an indoor training area for the Academy and work costing a considerable amount of money will commence within the next few months. This building is vital if we are to retain our Academy status.

2002

For the first time in 16 years we are back playing at the highest level in the world's greatest league, the FA Premiership. This was the end result of a remarkable season, the pinnacle of which was one of the most exciting days in the Club's history at Cardiff's Millennium Stadium where we beat Norwich City on penalties after extra time in the play-off final for the ultimate prize of promotion to the Premier League. The day was watched by a television audience of 6.5 million people, which was greater than for the FA Cup Final between Chelsea and Tottenham.

Since gaining promotion we have invested £7.1m in purchasing Robbie Savage, Aliou Cisse and Clinton Morrison. These players have made a significant impact on the team, showing that the manager has invested the Club's money well.

2003

We currently spend 54 per cent of our turnover on wages, but expect this percentage to increase as we continue to improve the playing squad and heighten our ambitions. The Board had hoped that the current strength of the squad would result in our not having to make any major investment in players until the summer of 2004. However with injuries to key personnel we may have to review this policy.

In the event that we do purchase additional playing staff this will have an immediate effect on wage costs. However the board is well aware of the need to find the right balance between risk and reward and will continue to manage your company's risk profile accordingly.

During December 2002 the Board made a decision that to avoid relegation we had to invest significantly in the team. We purchased Matthew Upson, Jamie Clapham and Steven [note: should be Stephen] Clemence, and we loaned Christophe Dugarry. These players made an instant impact on the team and we finished 13th in the Premier League. We also gained a place on the Premier League's tour of Malaysia along with Newcastle United and Chelsea. Total investment in players during the year exceeded £13m.

2004

During the year we spent £12m on players, which included the purchase of Martin Taylor, Maik Taylor, Julian Gray, Emile Heskey, Muzzy Izzet, Mario Melchiot, Jesper Gronkjaer and Dwight Yorke.

Sadly we lost the services through injury of Mikael Forssell early in the current season and consequently playing results suffered. We intend to go back into the transfer market during the January 2006 window with a view to strengthening the squad.

We are currently in discussions with Birmingham City Council about the possibility of a new 50,000 seater stadium being built by Las Vegas Sands INC with ourselves as anchor tenants. This project is driven by the desire for the city of Birmingham to have a multi-purpose stadium within the city, driving forward the ambitions of the Council to make Birmingham a destination location within Europe. The project is subject to Birmingham being granted one of the eight regional casino licences.

2005

Player amortisation costs showed a £2.4 million increase, up by 28.2 per cent. This increase arises from additional transfer fee payments crystallising for players already at the Club as a consequence of performance achievements being met, and further registration fees payable against players brought to the Club during the year. The Club invested £15.6m in players including the signings of Mikael Forssell, Jermaine Pennant, Walter Pandiani, Mehdi Nafti and Robbie Blake. Further investment has taken place in the playing squad during the January transfer window, seeing the arrival of Chris Sutton, Dudley Campbell and Martin Latka.

2006

When faced with relegation the Club took immediate action to alleviate the financial implications; in particular the annual wage bill was reduced by approximately £12 million with the release or sale of 13 first team squad players. Additionally, on the non-playing side, the Club made seven redundancies and did not renew the contracts of five other personnel. These reductions, together with some automatic salary adjustments to reflect non-Premier League status, made a further saving of £740,000.

During the close season we purchased players that we felt would give the Club the best chance of promotion at the end of the 2006/07 campaign. In order to finance this we sold Emile Heskey to Wigan and Jermaine Pennant to Liverpool for total fees of £12.2 million. This enabled us to acquire Cameron Jerome, Neil Danns, Stephen Kelly, Gary

McSheffrey, Raidi Jaidi, Bruno N'Gotty and Artur Krysiak at a combined cost of £8.6 million (costs to rise depending on the Club's success).

The Club also brought in on loan from Arsenal; Sebastian Larsson, Fabrice Muamba and Nicklas Bendtner, all of whom have had a beneficial effect on the team. The Club has an agreement in place with Arsenal to purchase the registration of Sebastian Larsson. More recently the Club also purchased the registration of Rowan Vine during the January 2007 transfer window for £2.5 million (further payments due dependent on the Club's success) and our captain Damien Johnson signed a new three-year contract.

2007

Everyone at the club is delighted to welcome Alex McLeish who has joined on a three and a half year contract, together with his management team of Roy Aitken and Andy Watson.

Plans to develop St Andrew's continue with enthusiasm and with the commitment of Birmingham City Council, with whom the Club has an excellent relationship. The redevelopment works at the Training Ground are now complete providing upgraded facilities for all age groups at the Club ranging from the Under 9s to the First Team.

We experienced a number of problems with the St Andrew's pitch during the year which resulted in the complete relaying of the surface. Thanks to the groundsman and his team's effort and hard work this has successfully eradicated the surface and drainage problems. For the last 12 months the combined expenditure on the Ground and Training facilities stands in excess of £2 million.

2008

Player amortisation rose from £8.4m in 2007 to £13.6m in the year to 31 August 2008 reflecting the write-off of additional costs incurred signing players in the 2007/08 pre-season and the January 2008 transfer window. In total during the period under review 14 senior players were sold or left the Club including Mikael Forssell, Fabrice Muamba and Olivier Kapo.

Significant profits were made on the sale of Muamba and Kapo to Wigan Athletic and Matthew Sadler to Watford while additional gains were made on performance targets achieved by players sold in previous years.

Senior players joining the Club during this time include James McFadden, David Murphy, Lee Carsley and Marcus Bent. In addition Kenny Agustain and Quincy Owusu-Abeyle have joined the Club for period on loan costing the Club in excess of £1.5 million.

The current season has started extremely positively with the Club recording the best ever start to a league campaign. The Club has been in the top two positions in the table since August. Games, particularly those at home have been very hard fought with many teams considering a visit to St Andrew's as their biggest game of the season. The Club has already been selected for eight appearances on Sky this season, the highest number of any Championship team, showing the strength and size of our brand.

The Club is undertaking scheduled major work on the Main Stand in 2008/09 costing in the region of £1.3m; this will involve a complete restructuring of the Stand and refurbishment of the Wiseman, Captain's Club and Trevor Francis areas.

2009

On 6 October 2009, Birmingham City plc, the company's immediate parent undertaking, was acquired by Birmingham International Holdings Limited (formerly Grandtop International Holdings Limited). On 11 November 2009, shares in Birmingham City plc were de-listed from the Alternative Investment Market.

2010

During the period, the Club was charged management fees of £280,000 by Roldvale Limited, a company of which D Sullivan is a director.

During the period, the Club was charged management fees of £280,000 by Gold Group International Limited, a company of which D Gold and R Gold are directors.

During the period, the Club advanced £12,096,264 (2009 – £Nil) in the form of a long-term loan from C Yeung, director. Interest of £234,057 (2009 – £Nil) was charged to the Club by C Yeung during the period. At the balance sheet date, £12,096,264 (31 August 2009 – £Nil) was due from the club to C Yeung and is included in creditors falling due after more than one year and £234,057 (31 August 2009 – £Nil) was due from the Club to C Yeung in respect of interest and is included in creditors falling due within one year. The loan carries interest at 5 per cent and has no fixed repayment date. During the period, the Club paid expenses on behalf of its ultimate parent undertaking Birmingham International Holdings Limited (formerly known as Grandtop International Holdings Limited) amounting to £2,533,175. At the balance sheet date £2,247,199 (31 August 2009 – £Nil) was due to the Club from BIHL and is included in debtors, amounts due from group undertakings.

Aggregate directors' emoluments include £940,831 received from Roldvale Limited for D Sullivan (31 August 2009 – £280,000 paid), £1,090,830 received from Gold Group International Limited in respect of D and R Gold (31 August 2009 – £280,000 paid) and £699,372 compensation for loss of office in respect of former director, K Brady.

2011

The balance sheet at 30 June 2011 shows net current liabilities of £44.7m (2010 £36.8m) and net liabilities of £19.2m (2010 – £6.9m). As at 30 June 2011 the Club received loans of £13.7m (2010 – £12.1m) from Yeung Ka Sing, Carson (a director of Birmingham City Football Club plc BCFC) and a director and substantial shareholder of the parent company BIHL and loans of £7.6m (2010 – £Nil) had been received from the parent company BIHL. This funding, combined with an overdraft facility which was utilised for the majority of the year to 30 June 2011, has provided the funding required to support the Club's operations.

Although technically repayable on demand the directors have received formal confirmation from Yeung Ka Sing, Carson and the parent company that, given the financial position of BCFC, the amounts due (or at least a significant element of the amounts due) to Yeung Ka Sing, Carson and the parent company will remain in place for at least the 12 months from the date of approval of these financial statements.

The bank overdraft facility was withdrawn as part of the annual review of the Club's banking facilities during August 2011 although the facility was not being used at that time. The directors would wish to once again thank all senior management at the Club who were able to sustain the Club's operations under these very challenging circumstances.

The directors note that allegations of dealing with property known or believed to represent the proceeds of an indictable offence during the period 2001 to 2007 have been made against the Club's biggest financial supporter Yeung Ka Sing, Carson by the Hong Kong police and that these allegations are currently progressing through due legal process in that jurisdiction. The first court hearing to consider the allegations has been tentatively rescheduled to take place in November of 2012.

At this stage of the proceedings the directors have not received any information to suggest that any funding provided to BCFC by Yeung Ka Sing, Carson either directly or through entities making payments to BCFC on his behalf were sourced from money laundered funds. Furthermore the directors do not have any credible reason to fear that the Hong Kong Authorities have any recourse to the loans made to BCFC by Yeung Ka Sing, Carson. As far as the directors are aware, only the assets located in Hong Kong are subject to an actual restrain.

Effective for 2011/2012 season the rights to the net income from the sponsorship of kit was transferred to a wholly owned subsidiary of the parent company, Birmingham (Hong Kong) Limited (BHK). The transfer was made on the basis of an informal and unwritten agreement between the directors of BCFC and BIHL ('common directors') to enable the HK-based company to maximise the potential of marketing the club within the Far East market. Given that this is a transfer between a wholly owned subsidiary and its parent, the parent company board requested that the transfer of these particular rights to be made at nil consideration.

The common directors consider that this transfer should not be regarded as a 'distribution in specie', which as BCFC have negative reserves could be deemed an illegal dividend as the underlying intention is to benefit the group as a whole from maximising the income received from the BCFC brand. BDO have advised that the UK tax authorities may seek to claim that this income (or receipt of funds in respect of the transfer of rights) should have been recorded by BCFC and therefore be subject to UK taxation. The common directors understand and accept this risk but are comfortable that there would be no impact to taxation to be recorded in the financial statement even if this was found to be the case by HMRC as a result of the significant tax losses carried within BCFC.

As a result of all the factors noted above it is appropriate that the net income generated from the sponsorship contract is recorded within the financial statements of BHK and that no income (either from sponsorship or on a transfer of rights) is recorded with the financial statements of BCFC. It is noted that Mr Pannu has throughout the audit given strong views to all material parties which have been considered by the parent board on this transaction. BDO have advised and it is confirmed that in the circumstances of this transaction it is appropriate to take advantage of the exemption conferred by the UK Financial Reporting Standard 8 'related party disclosures' not to disclose any details of this transaction or contract terms within the financial statements.

This issue alone has caused significant delay in publishing the accounts with the auditors having to seek appropriate clarifications from those concerned.

2012

The Directors can confirm that the parent company has been approached by three prospective buyers to explore the possibility of purchasing the Club. Discussions are at the advanced stage with one of the parties in Hong Kong although no binding agreement had been reached at this stage. All the prospective buyers have signed confidential non-disclosure agreements and the interested parties having sought and been provided with electronic due diligence materials in relation to the Club.

Following the departure of Mr Vico Hui from BIHL (effective from 1 July 2012) and BCFC (effective from 10 July 2012), the current directors have a better understanding of the Xtep deal. The deal was procured, negotiated and settled by Mr Vico Hui with the assistance of Mr Li Yiu Tung and Miss Pauline Wong, two other directors of BIHL. The original deal, signed between Birmingham (HK) Limited

('BHK'), a subsidiary of BIHL, was entered into by Mr Vico Hui with Xtep's subsidiary, Xtep (HK) Ltd, with the terms different from the second deal entered into by Mr Li Yiu Tung. It is understood that the original figures were different from the subsequent arrangement.

The second arrangement procured by Mr Hui with Xtep supported an arrangement whereby annual sponsorship payments from Xtep of HKD 16M, 17M, 18M, 19M and 20M (total of HKD 90M over five years) to be received. However, a so-called unannounced and undeclared counter sponsorship arrangement was also made whereby an annual figure of HKD 10M was to be repaid to Xtep, purportedly to support advertisements and promotion of BCFC/BIHL in China. The terms of the contract also states that the annual receivables were to come down by 50 per cent in the event of a relegation to the Championship, nevertheless, the counter sponsorship repayment to Xtep is to remain at HKD 10M per year, making the out flow larger than the sponsorship fee.

The current directors do not see any commercial sense in such an arrangement and the need for the counter payments of HKD 10M on an annual basis, particularly when the club is in the Championship which would produce negative return on an annual basis.

The Xtep deal ended on 18 June 2012 with Xtep pulling out following the issues raised during the last audit. Diadora is the new kit sponsor for the current season and all receivables are now booked into BCFC's accounts. Previous auditors, BDO LLP and BDO HK, had both resigned following the departure of Mr Vico Hui and a full review will be conducted on the Xtep deal by an independent consultant at BIHL level.

2013
The Directors are pleased to announce that during the year the Club's academy was awarded category 2 status under

the new Elite Player Performance Plan initiative. This is a great achievement which will hopefully see the continued production of quality young players from our academy. In establishing the category 2 status, the club has continued to invest in the infrastructure at the training ground with the construction of a brand new synthetic pitch having recently been completed.

2014

The company does not have an overdraft facility and meets its day to day funding requirements with support from the ultimate parent company, BIHL. In February 2014, as part of a debt restructuring programme ahead of the resumption of trading in BIHL shares on the Hong Kong stock exchange, a debt of £15.4 million owed by the company to Yeung Ka Sing, Carson was novated to BIHL.

As part of the debt restructuring programme, BIHL simultaneously released the company from its obligations to repay the replacement debt created by the novation. This has resulted in a capital contribution from BIHL to the company of £15.4 million which has been credited reserves in the year.

Bibliography

Karren Brady: *Karren Brady – Strong Woman – Ambition, Grit and a Great Pair of Heels* (Collins 2012)

Simon Jordan: *Be Careful What You Wish For* (Yellow Jersey 2012)

Barry Fry: *Big Fry – The Autobiography* (Collins Willow 2001)

Sam Allardyce: *Big Sam – My Autobiography* (Headline 2015)

Lou Macari: *Football, My Life – The Autobiography of a Sporting Legend* (Corgi Books 2008)

Karren Brady: *Brady Plays the Blues – My Diary of the Season* (Pavilion Books 1995)

David Gold with Bob Harris: *Pure Gold – My Autobiography – The Ultimate Rags to Riches Tale* (Highdown 2006)

Danny Dyer: *The World According to Danny Dyer – Tales From the East End* (Quercus 2015)

Tom Ross with Keith Dixon and David Salt: *The Game's Gone – My Autobiography* (DB Publishing 2016)

Steve Claridge: *Tales From the Boot Camps* (Orion 2000)

Dwight Yorke: *Born to Score* (Macmillan 2009)